PRAISE FOR *MINI PSYCHOLOGY*

'*Mini Psychology* made me smile and think. I even laughed out loud on several occasions ... As a schoolboy I once watched a film called *Physics Is Fun* presented by a very famous physicist of the day. Having watched the film, I wasn't so sure. This little book would persuade you that psychology is not just fun but hugely important.'

Professor Geoff Beattie, psychologist, author and broadcaster

'The most comprehensive – and delightful – guide to the human mind. Jonny Thomson delves into the most complex psychological topics and excavates their essence, using his signature warmth and curiosity to tell you exactly what you need to know to live a better life. This book will make you more empathetic, more self-aware and more effective in all that you do.'

Stephanie Harrison, author of *New Happy*

Jonny Thomson taught philosophy in Oxford for more than a decade before turning to writing full-time. He's a staff writer at Big Think, where he writes about philosophy, theology, psychology and anywhere he dares step out of his lane. He is the author of *Mini Big Ideas* and *Mini Philosophy*, an award-winning bestseller translated into twenty languages. Jonny also runs the 'Mini Philosophy' Instagram and Facebook accounts (@philosophyminis).

Jonny lives in Oxfordshire with his wife, who is very helpful, and his two young boys, who are not.

FURTHER PRAISE FOR JONNY THOMSON

'Engaging, smart and wise, *Mini Philosophy* is a diverse taster menu of ideas on life, the mind and the world.'
David Mitchell, author of *Cloud Atlas* and *The Bone Clocks*

'[*Mini Big Ideas* is] witty, knowledgeable and mind-expanding.'
Richard Fisher, author of *The Long View*

Mini Psychology

A Small Book About Our Big Brains

Jonny Thomson

WILDFIRE

First published in 2024 by
WILDFIRE
an imprint of HEADLINE PUBLISHING GROUP

1

Cataloguing in Publication Data is available from the British Library

Hardback ISBN 978 1 0354 1543 4

Typeset in Gotham by seagulls.net

Printed and bound in Great Britain by Clays Ltd, Elcograf S.p.A.

HEADLINE PUBLISHING GROUP
An Hachette UK Company
Carmelite House
50 Victoria Embankment
London EC4Y 0DZ

www.headline.co.uk
www.hachette.co.uk

To Mum and Dad — the therapist and
the psychologist.

Everyone needs good parents;
I got the best.

Contents

Introduction

Psychology is often mistaken for a modern discipline. People think it was invented in the cigar-fug of an Austrian café by men with names like Alfred Adler and Sigmund Freud. But humans have been doing a form of psychology for as long as we've been living together. For example, we have records of mental health diagnostics going back millennia, where people were described as 'melancholic', 'touched by the moon' (lunatic) or 'possessed'. Ancient scholars presented us with hugely detailed treatises on emotions, consciousness and rationality. Psychology has a rich, wide and long history.

My ambition with *Mini Psychology* is to demonstrate just how universal the subject is. On the one hand, this book will look at mainstream, modern theories of psychology, like those of Abraham Maslow, B. F. Skinner, Stanley Milgram, cognitive biases, conditioning and so on. On the other hand, we'll look at the historical and theoretical underpinnings of the subject, with the work of people like William James, Jean Piaget and John Locke.

But we'll also explore those curious stories and hidden nooks where you might not expect to find psychology. We'll look at computer games, social media and celebrity. We'll look at cult leaders torturing their acolytes and off-gridders hoarding tins of beans. We'll look at empathy, violence and how strange it is to be locked inside our private, cranial tower with no one to look at our thoughts.

Mini Psychology may be a short book but it explores the story of humanity itself. It teaches you all the important names and theories you need to know if you are studying the subject, while remaining grounded in the everyday reality of our lives. I hope you enjoy the journey inside your head half as much as I enjoyed writing it.

Clinical Psychology

Clinical psychology is when we try to understand what's going wrong and we try to fix it. It deals with how life is lived, and is concerned with the reality of emotions, trauma and mental illness. As opposed to a neuroscientific approach, clinical psychology treats the patient as a conscious being. It often involves talking therapies and counselling.

Clinical psychology is about helping people to be happy and whole.

Freud

It's Not About Your Mum (Kind of)

For many, childhood is a golden time. It's a period of security, happiness and blissful ease. If ever there is any problem, big or small, Mum or Dad can fix it. Your entire universe is a kind of pleasure palace, with parents satisfying all your needs. But then everything changes. Suddenly, we're ripped from this Edenic tranquillity and face the responsibilities, struggles and uncertainties of adulthood. We're told to deal with life and overcome obstacles ourselves. We look back on childhood and think, 'That was great.'

This is what Sigmund Freud argued, and his famous 'Oedipus complex' (named after the Greek tragic hero Oedipus, who kills his father and marries his mother) is much more complex than it is commonly, or wilfully, misunderstood to be.

Freud started out as a physiological psychologist, and after working with his patients he noticed particular themes emerging. His idea of the Oedipus complex was an attempt to explain these. In childhood, he argued, we have our desires and needs entirely met by our mother. She gives us life, nurses us and cares for us. In psychoanalytic terminology, she's the 'object' of our earliest self (meaning she's the thing that can satisfy our needs). But there comes a stage in our development when we realise that there is a rival, or an obstacle, to our mother's affection – our father. We notice that Mum has a separate, sexual life with Dad that we cannot be part of. There are borders to our pleasure palace and limits to the font of all happiness.

In discovering this, we learn we're not the entirety of our mother's world. The 'pre-Oedipal' halcyon days are gone and we are forced to nurture our own independence. We have to sleep in our own rooms, alone, while someone else gets the comfort of the 'object'. That pesky 'Dad' person.

So, the father is resented as the cause of our unwanted independence. We hate and envy him for his access to Mum. In an ideal world, we'd punch him, kick him and evict him. But it's complicated by the fact that Dad is also the authority figure. We cannot challenge him or remove him as an obstacle because he represents law and structure. So, we repress and internalise all those complicated feelings.

The Oedipus complex is not about men wanting to have sex with their mothers. It's much more subtle than that. In fact, these days, there's no reason why Mum needs to be the 'object' at all – it could be Dad or Grandma who is the primary caregiver, for instance. Freud's profound observation is that we all long for the wholeness and utter contentment that formed the basis of early childhood for most of us. And yet, however much we want these 'objects', life throws up obstacles and rivals to keep us at arm's length.

Beck and Ellis

CBT

When I was thirteen years old, my mum learned a new phrase. It was probably the most infuriating and teeth-grindingly frustrating thing you could say to any teenager: 'Choose your mood.'

My mum was a therapist and this was in the 1990s, so in hindsight, I think she must have just come back from a weekend top-up course in a new psychological fad: cognitive behavioural therapy (CBT). Today, CBT is widely considered to be one of the most successful and effective therapies there is. Which is why it's so popular.

In many ways, CBT is ancient Stoicism with a psychology degree. It's an empirically proven philosophy. The two main theorists behind CBT, Aaron Beck and Albert Ellis, explicitly said so. There are three elements that unite Stoicism and CBT.

The first is the notion of acceptance. This is where we have to have maturity and insight enough to recognise what things we can control and what things we can't. We cannot live forever. We cannot stop loved ones from dying. But we can live healthily and spend more time with our family. Change what you can and accept what you must.

The second is trust in our rationality. The Stoics believed that we could distance ourselves from our emotions. We could examine our moods. Likewise, modern cognitive-behavioural therapists believe we can step back a bit. We can pause and look inwards.

And stepping back is essential to the third element. This is the (infuriating) idea that we really can choose our mood. We can't choose our mood in the same way you might choose a tin of beans in the supermarket, but we *can* position our mind and our behaviour in such a way as to induce or dissolve certain feelings.

That all said, there is a danger of overworking the point. CBT is no doubt indebted to Stoicism but the two are not the same. CBT has evolved into a distinct therapeutic technique tailored to the complexities of modern mental health. It's a scientifically rigorous treatment plan and will often call on a range of techniques, including behavioural experiments, exposure therapy and mindfulness practices, which were not part of ancient Stoicism. But, most importantly, cognitive behavioural therapy explicitly focuses on our *behaviours* alone. It's about making us better at interacting with the world. It's about reducing anxiety, depression and much worse. It's a narrow, practical method to help us get by. Stoicism is much richer and fuller. It's a way of life with an overarching ethical code that seeks to *direct* your emotions and behaviours in a prescribed way.

At the end of the day, what matters for a lot of people is that CBT and Stoicism work. And they illustrate how philosophy is not just professors in shabby cardigans debating in ivory towers. It's a breathing, practical space where we can all grow and mend.

Ellis

You'll Get Through It

Human beings are a sturdy, resilient and heroic species. We've been through a lot and we'll go through a lot more yet. Dostoevsky once wrote that each of us is 'a creature that can get accustomed to anything'. And you are made of the same stern stuff as your forebears. You have made it to now. Every dark day and long night, every depressive, angry, miserable, sick moment of your life has been overcome, and you're still standing. You might not be a Russian novelist emerging from several years of Siberian exile, but you will persevere. You can get accustomed to anything.

This fact, this ability to withstand misery, is one of the three major adjustments necessary in Albert Ellis's rational emotive behaviour therapy (REBT).

Ellis's REBT starts with the premise that most of our emotional distress is caused not by external events but by our beliefs about those events. All of what we call suffering is actually due to our own perception. For example, imagine you are a highly devout, unwaveringly faithful religious believer. You see every action as an act of God. Like Job in the Old Testament, no matter how many misfortunes befall you, you'd take them in your stride as the test of a God who has your best interests at heart. Your underlying belief structure – your attitude towards the world – will affect how you process the events that happen to you.

Ellis believed that many people adopt irrational beliefs in how they approach the world, and these irrational beliefs amplify or even cause great misery. Ellis originally categorised eleven types of irrational belief, but modern REBT tends to coalesce around four major ones: demandingness (the belief that things must go a certain way), awfulising (the belief that something is worse than it is), low-frustration tolerance (the belief that one cannot stand something), and global evaluation (making one-off cases reflective of a rule).

Let's imagine Stephen comes in for REBT therapy. He says, 'My mum should talk to me more' (demandingness), 'She never really loved me' (awfulising), 'I don't think I can cope without my mum' (low-frustration tolerance), and 'My mum didn't even buy me a present last year. She'll never buy me a present' (global evaluation).

A standard therapy session with Stephen would involve teaching him how to identify his irrational beliefs, how to dispute them and how to develop effective coping strategies if they reappear. It involves letting him see that, like Dostoyevsky, Stephen *could* get by without his mum (but this might not be necessary anyway). REBT is about owning your attitude. It gives patients a label by which to recognise toxic beliefs. Once you can recognise a belief for what it is, you can take steps to disrupt and dispel it.

Everyday Psychology
Useful or Beautiful

You've just bought a new home. You've survived six months of unresponsive solicitors, packing boxes and cleaning the microbiomic ecosystem living behind your bookshelf. Now is the moment. You open the door to an entirely empty house. There are dust marks on the walls from pictures and furniture dents in the carpet, but the house is entirely void. It's minimalism on steroids – a home without *things*. It feels serene. Over the next few days, you will unpack your boxes. Every space will be filled. Empty walls will become busy. It's your home now, and it's nice to have a sofa, but that moment of calm is gone. The rooms seem smaller. The air is a little thicker. Your mind is a little cramped.

How we live will both reflect and affect our mental states. The spaces that we call home will change our mood – for better or worse.

In 1988, the American academic Russell Belk argued that our belongings act as extensions of our identities. He thought that our possessions not only reflect who we are but they also contribute to our sense of self. Our consumption habits define us. This includes not only tangible things, like a new dress or an iPhone, but also intangible possessions like memories, experiences and digital assets.

A key part of Belk's theory is what we buy for our homes. In 2007, Belk wrote an article specifically looking at Canadian tidiers and hoarders (who lived in clutter). He argued that living in a busy, messy state often provokes feelings of disgust, guilt, embarrassment and shame, which then lead a person to experience 'a disorganised life and a fragmented and chaotic sense of self'. In the years after the Second World War, the French philosopher Merleau-Ponty (see page 98) argued that our sense of 'being' cannot be abstracted from either our body or our place. The way you are thinking right now is affected, at least partially, by the objects around you.

The designer William Morris had a simple rule: 'Have nothing in your houses that you do not know to be useful or believe to be beautiful.' Everything else is clutter. It's a good principle, and one that many of us would do well to follow. But there's a part of our nature that just cannot. When it comes to throwing things away, many of us think, 'Oh, I might need that one day,' or, 'I can't throw this away; it reminds me of that great time I had!' In the back recesses of our brain there lies a tiny hoarder, clutching onto holiday souvenirs and pasta rollers like Gollum.

But what Belk argued is that we should be wary of the hoarding tendency. A busy, cluttered and claustrophobic house will affect your mental health. A tidy house really does mean a tidy mind.

Jung

More than a Coincidence

The *I Ching* (or *The Book of Changes*) is a 3,000-year-old divination tool. It contains sixty-four hexagrams – symbols made up of six lines each. It's thought that the hexagrams represent the dual aspects of the universe: some lines are broken (yin) and others are whole (yang). A prospective soothsayer will, after following some complex rules, give you a series of hexagrams. For example, you might get the Abysmal (#29), representing the dangerous abyss, the Marrying Maiden (#54), representing a union which might not be equal, and Gnawing Bite (#27), representing teeth coming together to resolve a problem.

Armed with your hexagrams, you go away and reflect. What could the three hexagrams together represent? What can they tell you about your life? What do the Marrying Maiden, the Gnawing Bite and the Abyss have in common? Within the wider theological framework of the *Book of Changes*, your hexagrams are a kind of cleromancy – a divinely inspired message. Guidance from the Dao.

But for the Swiss psychoanalyst Carl Jung, the *I Ching* is an example of synchronicity.

For Jung, synchronicity is when we see two causally unrelated things as meaningfully connected in some way. Suppose, for instance, that you had a recurring dream about an old school friend – a friend you've not seen for a long time. Then, by coincidence, you see that friend in the supermarket while travelling in a new city. Synchronicity is a bit more than 'Oh, that's weird'; it's something that forces you to reconsider your own psyche or even the world. It's something that says: 'There must be something to this – I'm going to reconnect with this friend.'

How much spiritual or quasi-religious emphasis Jung put on this is a subject of much debate. His own interest in the *I Ching* implies that he was at least open to the idea of some kind of cosmic hand behind this synchronicity. But for our purposes, synchronicity is best understood as a psychotherapeutic tool. In analytic psychology, these coincidences are seen as moments where the unconscious forces itself onto the conscious. It's a desperate scream to be heard from the subliminal, psychodynamic forces within you. Synchronicity feels spiritually true because it carries the weight of your entire unconscious. Seeing your friend in the supermarket seems like it's 'meant to be' because it's your unconscious finally being recognised.

Synchronicity does, undoubtedly, occupy a corner in the unfalsifiable kingdom of pseudoscience. It's untestable. But even if you see Tarot cards, divination, horoscopes, dreams and the *I Ching* as quackery, it's true to say that often great, life-changing revelations can be born of them. The unconscious, for Jung, cannot speak, so it resorts to abstract symbols, nudges and interpretative dance. Do not ignore the coincidences in life. They might be trying to tell you something.

Skinner

You Are a Pigeon

If you've ever played a gambling game on your phone or dropped some coins into a one-armed bandit, you'll have been amazed at how close you came to winning. Five times in a row, you nearly won the big jackpot. If only that cherry could be nudged a little higher, then it would be drinks on you at your new mansion. So, you press 'PLAY' again or put another coin in the machine.

A distant, muffled part of your psyche knows the game is rigged, but it doesn't matter. Your heart is racing, your blood is up and your hand is twitching at the prospect of your winnings. Somewhere, far away in *their* mansions, are the clever psychologists who designed those games. They've spent decades programming them to condition you to play more. They're brainwashing devices, with garish lights and loud noises. To all those gambling barons, you are like a pigeon in a box, pecking away in the hope of getting food that never arrives.

And it's all down to the American behaviourist B. F. Skinner and his work on operant conditioning.

Since the dawn of parenting, humans have known on some level about conditioning. If you praise good behaviours, a child will do more of them. If you punish the bad behaviours, they stop (or learn to hide them). In the 1950s and 1960s, Skinner turned folk knowledge into scientific fact. He conducted a series of experiments on pigeons and rats and discovered that if you reward certain behaviours, like giving a rat food as it pushes a lever, the animal will carry on doing it. Somewhat darkly, it's since been shown that when you then stop giving food at the push of the lever, a rat will carry on pushing away and starve to death even if other food is available. The cages where Skinner conditioned his animals were known as 'Skinner boxes'.

One of the more curious of Skinner's discoveries was about superstitions. Occasionally, Skinner would give food to a pigeon at random. It might be when the pigeon pushed a lever, but it could also happen at any time. The pigeons started to develop all sorts of strange, superstitious behaviours. Without any obvious 'this action causes this outcome', they resorted to guesswork. The birds would bow, jump, peck, twirl, coo or whatever because they assumed there must be some kind of causal connection they just couldn't find. It begs the question of how pigeon-like many human superstitions may be.

Skinner's work might have been obvious in some ways, but it is the bedrock of a lot of consumer and educational psychology. School behaviour contracts, aversion therapy, smartphone apps, token economies and casinos are all built around Skinner's work. We all live in a glorified Skinner box.

Everyday Psychology
Cult Leaders and Abusive Relationships

Roch Thériault was an intelligent and charismatic religious extremist who, in the 1970s, founded a commune known as the Ant Hill Kids in the woods around Quebec. He insisted his followers were 'free of sin' and used violence and abuse to keep people in check. He would make them eat dead mice and faeces, and punished people by breaking their legs or cutting off their toes. He tortured and murdered children.

Few ever left the Ant Hill Kids. One, Gabrielle Lavallée, tried, but she went back of her own volition when she couldn't handle life outside. She had her arm amputated as punishment. In 1989, Thériault was finally arrested and imprisoned, ten years after he began his horrific doomsday cult.

Why do cults attract such obsessive and fanatical loyalty? What tricks do cult leaders use to woo their followers? And how susceptible are you and I to joining a cult? If we look at the various psychological literature and sociological studies, we can pick out three main techniques.

First: isolation. It's hugely important that a new cult member be cut off from their family and friends. There can be no voice from the outside world to say, 'Are you sure self-mutilation is a good idea?' or 'Have you got any evidence the world's going to end on Friday?' Cults make sure to fill your every moment and every day with the same message from like-minded fanatics. There's little room for doubt or introspection.

Second is a trick called a 'love bomb'. New recruits are often showered with affection. Their every whim is met, and the commune resembles nothing less than an Edenic retreat. The apocalyptic cult the Children of God even used a technique known as 'flirty fishing', where members would deliberately enter sexual relationships with potential converts. It is thought that over 200,000 potential converts were 'fished' this way.

The third is fear. The British philosopher Thomas Hobbes once argued that of all human emotions, fear was the most powerful. Love comes close but lacks the motivational clout of cold terror. With cults, there are two kinds of fear: the first is ostracisation. A cult quickly becomes *everything* to its members, so being outcast would be disastrous. The second is the real fear of pain and punishment.

Using these techniques, cults will break down your sense of self and any notion of true or false, right or wrong. They then fill these gaps with cult dependency and the promise of salvation. You're broken; we can fix you. You have nowhere to go; we can offer you a home. No one wants you; we are your family.

In fact, most kinds of emotional manipulation rely on these techniques. If someone can make you feel insecure, incomplete and inadequate, then they can present themselves as the solution. That happens not just in cults but in abusive relationships of every kind.

Perls

The Past is the Past

Susan is an idiot. She's a rude, selfish and duplicitous narcissist. Sadly, she's also Harry's auntie, and so Harry can't get Susan out of his life. Every Christmas, Susan is there, casting her shadow and grinding his gears. And on Boxing Day every year, Harry turns to his wife and says, 'Christ, Susan's an idiot.'

When you meet people like Susan, all is not what it seems. No one is born with horns and a pitchfork; no baby is evil. Something has made Susan who she is. The question, then, is: how far should we frame Susan's behaviours as the understandable manifestation of a miserable childhood, and how much should we judge her unpleasantness in the here and now?

It's a question not only for Harry but for psychotherapy more broadly. When we are trying to treat someone, should we dig in and unpack their past or treat them as they are today? Of course, no therapy is ever entirely this or that, but broadly speaking, Freudianism seeks to unpack and resolve our past tensions, while CBT and gestalt therapy focus much more on what we have now.

Gestalt therapy, which is different from gestalt psychology (see pages 98–9), is what happens when critics get organised. It began, essentially, as a criticism of Freudianism and eventually became its own school entirely. The German psychiatrist Fritz Perls started out as a huge fan of Freud. He saw a lot to like in the ideas of the unconscious and psychodynamic forces, but he found two main problems. Problems that gestalt therapy sought to avoid.

The first problem for Perls was that Freud placed too much emphasis and spent too much clinical time on the past. You could spend a year's salary to lie on a chaise longue and talk about your emotionally unavailable father without ever actually improving your life today. Perls didn't necessarily disagree that resolving past conflicts would heal you in the now, but it took valuable time. Instead, gestalt therapy invites clients to experience and understand their *current* feelings, thoughts and behaviours. It's less 'Tell me about your mother' and more 'Right, your mother did that; how can we move on?'

The second problem Perls saw in Freudianism was that it focused too much on adaptation and normalisation. Freud was all about finding a balance in the world, but Perls believed that we also bring a bit of ourselves to the world. We are made by our environments, but we construct them, too. We are creative, driven and trailblazing explorers. Sometimes we walk a well-trodden path and sometimes we bushwhack a new way with heroic gumption. Gestalt therapy, then, is less about resolution or peace and more about finding your own route through life.

Arguably, gestalt therapy has not gone away but rather been enveloped into the efficacious arms of CBT (see pages 16–17). With its emphasis on individual responsibility, choice and self-examination, gestalt therapy was an essential path to a truly therapeutic talking treatment. And it means Harry can call out Susan for being an idiot.

Rogers

A Good Friend and a Good Therapist

'The King Lindworm' is a Danish fairy tale about a huge, hungry lindworm. He is betrothed to various maidens and princesses – high and mighty woman, with great dowries and beauty – and he eats them all. He gobbles them up with serpentine greed. Then, one day, a shepherd's daughter comes to be married to the lindworm. After the formalities, they find themselves alone in the bedchamber. The lindworm tells the young woman to take off her dress so he can eat her. She replies, 'Only if you shed a skin.' He is surprised, but he does so. She takes off her dress, only to reveal another dress beneath, like some petticoated Russian doll.

'Take off your dress,' the worm says.

'Only if you shed a skin,' she replies. On and on it goes until, eventually, the lindworm has shed skin enough to reveal what lies beneath – a handsome and loving prince.

Of course, you can interpret 'The King Lindworm' any way you like, but it's a good analogy for the reward of psychoanalysis. The shedding of our tough, unwanted skin reveals a whole, happy, inner self that is buried under the hard things in life.

The American Carl Rogers disliked psychotherapeutic systems. Rogers thought that any therapist with a tick sheet or a method was more likely to damage their patient than heal them. A square hole is good for some people, but most people aren't squares. Instead, Rogers developed his 'person-centred therapy', which emphasises the importance of providing a supportive therapeutic environment where clients can achieve self-actualisation. The approach is grounded in concepts of unconditional positive regard, empathy and congruence.

There are two basic assumptions at the core of Rogers' theory: first, we each want to self-actualise, to be whole on our own terms. Second, only we, the individual, know how we can realistically do that. The role of the psychotherapist, then, is not to 'fix' the patient or to tell them X or Y, it's to listen, elicit and guide. The princesses cannot tell the lindworm to be human; it requires the shepherd's daughter to facilitate his deskinning.

For Rogers, good therapy requires some 'necessary and sufficient conditions' designed to develop an open, accepting and warm relationship between the therapist and the client (Rogers always used the word client). The therapist must be whole in themselves (i.e., they must be psychologically stable and healthy enough to help another person). They must also be entirely unjudgemental.

In many ways, the ideal Rogerian therapist is like a good friend or partner. They listen. They accept you. They do not try to tell you what to do or what you've done wrong; they ask open questions and invite you to explore your own psychology. We all have a whole, happy, human inside of ourselves – we just need the right person to help us reveal it.

Linehan

Sometimes Life Can Be Rubbish

Most therapy begins with an underlying assumption: the client has a problem that can be fixed. Here is the issue, here is the solution; let's bring them together. Sometimes, though, the problems cannot be resolved, the neuroses cannot be talked away. Sometimes we just have to *live* with things.

This 'radical acceptance' is an essential part of dialectical behaviour therapy (DBT). DBT is a strange mixture of Buddhist theology, Hegelian philosophy and modern science, brought together by the American psychologist Marsha Linehan. In some ways, it's CBT (see pages 16–17) plus a few extra bits. But those extra bits are enough to make it fascinating in its own right. The 'dialectical' part of DBT comes from the dialectic method of Georg Hegel, which involves a thesis (one position), an antithesis (an opposite or conflicting position) and then a synthesis (some kind of resolution or compromise). DBT asks us to look closely at the synthesis part.

Anyone with emotional maturity beyond a toddler's appreciates that we have to compromise in life. We must give a little to get a little. But compromise can be rubbish. No one is entirely happy, and we just have to deal with it. DBT asks us to compromise with our own contradictions. On page 58, we look at the concept of cognitive dissonance – the idea that humans hate holding conflicting beliefs at any one time. Usually we jettison or downplay one of the offending beliefs. Linehan's DBT, however, argues that we inevitably *will* hold conflicting beliefs. Life is hard – sometimes *very* hard – but that's just life.

Like CBT, DBT places great emphasis on being honest with ourselves and looking in on our thoughts. It's about taking control of the narrative in your head and reframing your attitude to your feelings. It differs from CBT, though, in that it underlines something called 'distress tolerance'. Linehan herself explains this best when she writes: 'The path out of hell is through misery. By refusing to accept the misery that is part of climbing out of hell, you fall back into hell.'

Linehan's point – a structural principle of DBT – is that we will all need a degree of mental and physical resilience if we're to get through life. We need to accept that things will be hard sometimes, but we can either endure those times or deal with them. A lot of therapies, like Freudianism, for example, often assume there is a 'right' way to live and that if we reach that stage, there'll be no more problems. DBT is about embracing your shortcomings, accepting the bad things, and getting used to living with contradiction.

Bowlby
Someone at Your Back

Grace and Edward sit at opposite ends of the sandpit. They do not know each other. When you're four years old, you don't know many people. They are both shy but curious. And so there they sit, staring at one another. After a while, Grace makes the first move. She sidles into the middle of the sandpit and picks up a bucket. Edward looks at his dad before dropping himself down onto the sand. The next five minutes are a carefully choreographed ceremony of bum shuffling and gradual proximity. Grace moves in a bit, and Edward leans closer. Within ten minutes, the two are playing like old friends.

For the British psychoanalyst John Bowlby, Grace and Edward have developed secure 'attachment styles'.

Bowlby believed that all humans have an 'attachment system' that seeks comfort, support and love. A child instinctively seeks a bond with their parent, and how that bond forms will define their attitude towards attachment in later life. Bowlby believed that if our attachment system is satisfied and we know we have the backing of our caregivers then our 'exploratory system' is turned on. We feel confident enough to strike out. Grace hops into the sandpit because she *knows* her mother is there, somewhere. She feels secure and looked after, so she shuffles over to Edward. Edward is a bit more reticent in that he looks back at his dad to check if he's there, and Bowlby would say this is an 'anxious-ambivalent' attachment style.

According to Bowlby, everyone you meet will fit one of four attachment styles. Secure people, who have had love growing up, often form relationships easily and have the self-confidence to explore. Anxious-ambivalent people have had some degree of attachment, but it is irregular or conditionally given. They distrust relationships and often enter them fearing eventual abandonment: 'You'll leave me, just like my dad did!' Most people are one of these two.

Sadly, some children do not get adequate love at all, and grow up to be either 'avoidant' or 'disorganised'. Avoidant people have become so used to looking after themselves that they find it very hard to let anyone in and allow themselves to appear vulnerable. They think they don't need anyone because they never had anyone. Disorganised attachment is worse still, and it will be violent and destructive. Disorganised people won't only avoid others, they will push them away if there's a risk of being attached.

Bowlby's attachment theory is not only intuitively appealing (we all know people who fit one of his four attachment styles) but has been empirically proven by the likes of Mary Ainsworth (see page 88) and others since. It reinforces the idea that we are all simply the product of our upbringing. We are what we learn, and if we learn one form of attachment, then that's the model for how we'll live.

Winnicott
Willy the Weasel

Most children play with toys, and kids will often drag around with them some beloved, bedraggled, knitted curiosity. The early connections children have with these toys are intense and important. Woe betide the family that leaves behind Willy the Weasel at the holiday home – they will have to either turn around or tolerate three hours of screaming in the car plus a week of broken nights.

Why are these early toys or objects so important to children? For the English psychoanalyst Donald Winnicott, it's because they play the role of 'transitional object'.

According to most theories of psychotherapy, in very early infancy, a child cannot differentiate themselves from their primary caregiver (usually a mother, but not necessarily). Whenever the child feels some internal desire, such as for milk, a cuddle or pain relief, the mother is there to provide what is needed. From the outside, it looks like the mother is reading the child's mind. From the perspective of the child, it's as if the mother is *inside* their mind. The mother is an appendage like a hand that knows what the child wants.

Then, over time, the child starts to realise that the mother is a separate thing. Children start to navigate the distinction between 'me' and 'not me' and develop a capacity for very rudimentary forms of self-regulation. But this transition is not easy, and it can be traumatic for the child. Traumatic, but ultimately beneficial. To make the process less painful, a child will use a 'transitional object', like a toy. The transitional object is subsumed by the child; it's imagined to be *part* of the child, just like the mother once was. So, the toy now provides comfort, as the mother used to. The child can call upon the transitional object as a balm for anxiety and to provide security when they feel alone. It's why, Winnicott argued, transitional objects are particularly important to the child at times of insecurity or anxiety, like at bedtime or in the dark.

The notion of 'transitional objects' fits into Winnicott's wider 'object relations' theory, where a child often comes to use objects (which can include people) to satisfy some desire. They learn that they can use parts of the world to solve their problems and that Mum or Dad are only part of that world.

Winnicott's theory suffers in the same way that all psychoanalysis does: it's hard to study, harder to replicate and impossible to really prove. There's no way to test or discover how an early-stage infant identifies with their mum or a toy. A six-month-old can't even crawl, let alone reflect and self-report on their various psychodynamic forces. But for all that, Winnicott's theory seems plausible. It's a good explanation for a common phenomenon, and, in the absence of any other provable theory, it's as good as any out there.

Everyday Psychology
Emu-tional Support

When Nicholas Olenik's brother died, he found himself tumbling through a downward spiral of grief, depression and loneliness. Struggling under a looming mental health crisis, Olenik reached out to one of his close friends for support. His friend listened to everything Olenik said and, after a long pause, said, 'Hey, buddy, why don't you get an emu?'

Olenik bought an emu egg, raised the chick and the two fell in love. Every day, Olenik would take Nimbus the emu on a walk, and his mental health got better and better. Sadly for Olenik, emus were not on the Virginia Beach General District's list of approved livestock. So, when Olenik was caught walking Nimbus along the seashore, enjoying the lapping waves, he was given a $50 fine and told never to take his emu out again. Olenik fought back, and eventually all parties came to an agreement: Nimbus could live on a ranch with other emus, and Olenik could move in with him. A happy man living with his happy bird.

The story of Nimbus and Olenik hit the news in 2023 but it is a tale as old as time. For millennia, humans have kept pets – from dogs and cats to emus and geckos – and they make us happier and make life feel a bit fuller.

In 1880, Florence Nightingale tried everything humanly possible to make her Crimean patients better. In her *Notes on Nursing*, she observed that people in a room with a caged bird often felt more relaxed and less in pain. What Nightingale observed, science has confirmed. In several studies since the 1980s, it's been proved that keeping pets reduces the chances of a heart attack, makes you less likely to get ill, and leaves you better equipped to deal with stress (see pages 258–9). Pets reduce cortisol levels, lower blood pressure, alleviate isolation, generate feelings of social support and enhance happiness.

So, there's a lot of evidence to suggest that having pets at least correlates with improved wellbeing. It's hard to prove conclusively because having a pet also involves a lot of confounding behaviours. Walking a dog, for example, involves exercising, being outside and demonstrating care, all of which are proven to enhance mental health. The 'biopsychological' model of wellbeing argues that our biology, social network and psychology are interlinked so much that if you tinker with one, you affect the others. Owning a pet expands your social circle. Pets act as friends and supporters. They are always there, unjudging and loyal, and are on your side. Except cats, who want to kill you.

Whether it's Nicholas and Nimbus frolicking on their Virginian ranch or a dog's wagging tail and excited jumps when its owner comes home, pets are an essential part of a lot of people's personal wellbeing.

Mahler

Setting Out into the World

One of the defining elements of growing up is learning how to fend for yourself. There comes a time in life when we realise that our home is far too small and the world is far too big to stay put. It's what makes us pick up the backpack and step out – that moment when an itchy-footed would-be hero crosses a threshold. Almost all the stories we tell involve a transition from a state of naïve, childish dependency to adulthood.

And this transition happens long before our teenage identity crisis (see pages 108–9). It happens in the first months and years of our lives. It rewires our brains and redefines who we are. This is what Margaret Mahler called 'separation-individuation'.

According to Mahler, we can identify definite steps in the first moments of a child's life as they change from a blinking, crying, puffy baby into a running, playing, socialising toddler. When a baby is first born, they are said to belong to the 'normal autistic stage' of life, largely unaware of the external world. After a few weeks, in the 'symbiotic stage', the baby recognises that the mother (or other primary caregiver) exists, not as a separate thing (see page 36) but as an appendage. Mum is a need-fulfilling limb, far better than the baby's own flailing, useless ones.

Then come differentiation and separation. At around half a year, the baby realises first that Mum and then the world are independent objects to be interacted with. The child experiments. They bash and grab. They put things in their mouth. From now until toddlerhood, there is a cautious exploratory ballet known as 'ambitendency', where a child will try out new things but then come running back to the mother. All of which culminates in 'object constancy', where the child has internalised the love and support of their caregiver and will go on to independent childhood.

Ernest Hemingway once wrote: 'To be a successful father, there's one absolute rule: when you have a kid, don't look at it for the first two years.' When I first heard that, I thought a bit less of the old man of the sea. But if you read Hemingway through the lens of Mahler, you see he's got a point. For Mahler, writing in the early twentieth century, the mother represents care and sustenance. The father embodies the exciting, independent and dangerous external world. If Mahler is right, a very young child has no need for the father figure; he represents an independent world the child can't even conceptualise, let alone interact with.

Of course, people no longer talk in such gender-stereotypical terms. But Mahler does offer a compelling explanation of a documented phenomenon: for a long period of early development, children focus only on the home and the caregivers. Their immediate surroundings are their entire universe.

Cognitive Psychology

Cognitive psychology steps inside the brain to see what it's up to. It focuses on the various mental processes that make up the brain's daily work. Sometimes it homes in on one, such as memory, and at other times it focuses on the wider picture to see how the mechanisms interact.

Cognitive psychology is about cognitive processes like attention, problem solving or creativity.

Atkinson and Shiffrin
Incompetent Geniuses

You are walking along the street and a car flashes past you. You get a glimpse of colour and hear a swish of sound. You turn your attention to the road and focus on a second car; it turns off at the next junction. When your walking companion asks you what kind of car it was, you say a red Ferrari. Then, in a moment of trauma-flecked flashback, you remember that you were knocked off your bike on this very road a few years ago.

You have just used the three types of memory proposed by cognitive psychologists such as Richard Atkinson, Richard Shiffrin and, more recently, Alan Baddeley and Graham Hitch (see page 48). The multi-modal model of memory describes three areas. The first is a sensory register lasting about one to two seconds, briefly noticing echoic (auditory), iconic (visual) and haptic (touch) features. The second is working memory, or short-term memory, lasting about six to twelve seconds and with a limited capacity. Third, there is long-term memory, which (potentially) lasts indefinitely if you have even a degree of the organisation necessary for recall and retrieval.

So, in your walk, you used sensory memory to recall the first car going past, working memory to recall the second car as it went around the corner, and long-term memory to retrieve the information about your accident.

Of course, being cognitive-psychological models, things are not as simple as that. Working memory is divided into a 'visuospatial' sketchpad, an 'acoustic store' and an 'articulatory loop'. In our example above, we have an image of the car, the growling of the engine and the formulation of the sentence to tell your companion.

Long-term memory is no less confusing and tends to be divided into three parts, too. We have *episodic* memories, which are episodes or things in your life you remember (see page 60). *Semantic* memory is your knowledge of the world – words, trivia and so on. Both of these would have been used in remembering and then recounting your accident. Third, *procedural* memory is how to do things. It could be complex things like the stages in making a curry or operating heavy machinery, or simple things like turning a door knob. It's mostly thought that long-term memory alters our RNA at the cellular level. It's deeply engraved, but not always easy to access.

There is a lot of memory going on in your head. Nothing about cognitive psychology is straightforward, and the processes that we use for one 'type' of memory often bear little similarity to others. You might have a great semantic memory but it takes you months to learn any new procedural skill. You can go to Oxford to study astrophysics without knowing how to tie a shoelace.

James

The Fringe

Let's spend some time inside our heads. Imagine your mind is a cavernous room, and lying jumbled this way and that are all the objects of your consciousness. Take a look around. Walk from piece to piece, place to place. Stay and look at a particular memory, feeling, sensation or piece of trivia. Breathe in what you see, like a critic at a gallery. But what's this? In the corner, there's a big, murky fog. Or a mysterious shape, covered in a sheet. There's a door with a question mark on it. A deep hole with no end. These, too, are in your mind's room.

These places embody what the American thinker William James calls the 'fringe' of the mind.

James is a mainstay of psychology, but his works are so philosophical that he can't be easily defined. One key idea in his 1892 book *The Stream of Consciousness* is how the mind is not simply made up of 'substantive' aspects, like the objects in our room. These 'resting places', which are usually 'occupied by sensory imaginations', are common, and they're dominant, but they're not the full picture. There are also 'transitive' aspects of our consciousness that move us between thoughts. There are cities and roads connecting them. But we cannot 'stop them to look at them' because to do so is to annihilate them. It will turn the transitive into the substantive.

The strange thing, though, is that we sometimes do catch ourselves looking at an absence. This is the so-called 'fringe'. Suppose, for instance, I say, 'Wait!' You are, at that moment, kept in limbo for some new, incoming experience. Or, if you are trying to remember a name or a fact for a quiz, your mind scans itself like a prison camp's searchlight, hoping against hope to stumble on the answer. Our minds are made up of expectations and anticipation. We're ready for something, even if that something is unknown. The mind is sometimes an empty glass waiting to be filled.

James's point is that the mind cannot be reduced to the objects contained within it, any more than a river can be reduced to a simple number of litres of water. As James says: 'Every definite image in the mind is steeped and dyed in the free water that flows around it.' The mind is a stream. The mind is the person wandering around the room, as much as the objects contained within.

Baddeley and Hitch
The Crack Team of the Brain

There have been some budget cuts. We can't afford *Ocean's Eleven* so we're down to *Ocean's Three*. A crack team of three individuals, masters in their fields, and slick as George Clooney in a tailor-made tux. First, we have Sketchpad: he's the art guy. Give him an idea and he'll doodle it out in seconds. Next up, we've got Phonoloop: she's the Sherlockian savant. If you reel off the books of the Old Testament, she'll have them noted as fast as you can say them. Then we have C-Ex: he's the boss of this operation, the man with the plan.

This is *Ocean's Three: Short-Term Memory*, as conceived by Alan Baddeley and Graham Hitch.

In 1974, Baddeley and Hitch did some revolutionising. For a long time, the psychology of memory worked on a pretty simplistic model of long- and short-term memory, with not much expansion on what those actually meant. Your short-term memory (STM) is, essentially, the ability to hold facts or learn skills just long enough to use them. If you frantically revise some statistic outside the exam hall, use it in an essay and then forget it forever after, that's your STM. It's all about churn and burn. What Baddeley and Hitch did was to unpack exactly what's going on here.

They suggested there were (at least) three elements to our STM.

First there's the *visuospatial sketchpad.* You make yourself a coffee in the morning and put it down. You pop off to put the laundry out to dry, you go to the toilet and you open the kids' curtains. Where is your coffee? That ability to remember where things are – to paint a temporary map of the world – is your sketchpad.

The *phonological loop* is your ability to remember things you hear, usually speech, as well as the 'voice' you hear in your head while reading. Let's test your phonological loop. Read this:

There was a pink dog talking to an angry bird eating a jiggling fish as a brown whale splashed grey foam on pink rocks.

Without looking back, what colour was the dog? How good is your loop?

Finally, the *central executive* uses the information from the other two. It walks you to your coffee or writes down a fact you crammed. It takes the information from the previous sentence and applies it to this. Peanuts in the morning. That sentence was jarring, wasn't it? Well, your central executive is the one who called it out.

I've got two young children, and you can say what you like about them but they put my STM to the test. They distract, overwhelm and deafen my sketchpad and phonological loop. Which is why, when I make myself a coffee these days, I have no idea where I left it.

Everyday Psychology
The Seeking System

All great adventures start with curiosity. All of the best stories begin this way, too. Jack climbs a beanstalk to find out what's at the top. Bluebeard's wife is allowed in any room but one, and so she obsesses over what's inside. And, of course, in Genesis, God tells Adam to do what he wants, but just don't eat that one thing.

Curiosity is often the driving force behind all science. It has us explore the moon, climb the highest mountains and map the deepest oceans. But it's also our downfall. It's the voice that says 'push the button' or 'lick that frozen pole'. It melted Icarus's waxen wings.

When it comes to curiosity, we are not born equal. Some people can't help but probe and investigate. Others are quite happy with what's in front of them. So why isn't curiosity more universal across the species? It's all to do with what the Estonian-American neuroscientist Jaak Panksepp called our 'seeking system'.

For Panksepp, the seeking system is what makes a person explore beyond their comfort zone. It is a goal-oriented system that says, 'Here is the target, and here's the reward if you hit it.' The seeking system is an evolutionary mechanism that pushes humans to be risk-seekers. Without the seeking system, we'd just sit in our den, content with whatever meagre lot we have.

On a neurological level, this is all thanks to our 'mesolimbic pathway'. When you satisfy a desire or curiosity, a part of your brain called the ventral tegmental area pumps out dopamine. This hormone is then whisked along a pathway to the orbitofrontal cortex, located near the front of your brain. This is then translated into 'Ooooh, yeah!'

As a child grows up, their brains will naturally reward them for risk-seeking behaviours. It hands out dopamine prizes to the curious and adventurous in the room. Anyone who's lived with a teenager will know how frustrating their constant boundary-pushing can be. But this is what they're wired to do – it's what allowed us to forage for food, find new and better pastures, and progress as a species. If a teenager is successful in satisfying their curiosity or is allowed to indulge it more often, they will establish certain curiosity pathways later in life. So, if a child is given exciting environments to explore, a room to play and experiment in, or the freedom to ask questions and investigate, then they will do so more later in life.

Of course, the nature vs. nurture debate (see page 82) will not go away overnight. Genetics and natural brain composition will still be factors for many. But the more a reward pathway is encountered in risk-seeking or curiosity, the more it will be used again.

Chomsky

Can We Beat Human Language?

Unless you've been entirely unplugged for two years or make a conscious effort to avoid all technology news, you've probably heard of ChatGPT or large language models (LLMs). At the end of 2022, OpenAI unveiled ChatGPT 3, which could write university-quality essays and create Shakespearean sonnets about cars, and often passed the Turing Test (in being indistinguishable from a human conversationalist). Fast forward to now, and we have ChatGPT 4, Claude 3 and Google's Gemini – all of which make ChatGPT look like a fumbling preschooler. By the time you read this, ChatGPT 5 has probably saved the world, or destroyed it, depending on your perspective.

In the space of a year, human language and creativity has gone from bordering on the divine to bested by an algorithm. But, according to Noam Chomsky, humans still have a trick or two left.

In my earlier book *Mini Philosophy*, I looked at Chomsky's nativist theory of language. Essentially, Chomsky suggests that humans have an innate ability to learn language, which he explains with the concept of the 'universal grammar'. Chomsky argues that children *naturally* acquire language without explicit instruction due to this built-in predisposition. There's an innate structure to our brains that allows us to understand the depth, variety and nuances of semantics (meaning) and syntax (the way words work).

Studies showing how children can master two or three hugely complex, and linguistically unrelated, languages by the age of four suggest that language is something we're born to be good at. Evolutionarily, that makes sense. We need to communicate to collaborate. We need to collaborate if we're to beat all those big animals and terrifying storms.

But suddenly, AI has made us look Neanderthalic. AI can learn every language there is in the time it takes to study some training data. It can easily become fluent, competent and creative in other languages – and it doesn't take four years. It takes less than four minutes. So, do humans still have an innate universal grammar?

In March 2023, Chomsky wrote an article arguing that LLMs are 'basically high-tech plagiarism'. They are good for descriptions and predictions but not causal explanations. He called AI 'a lumbering statistical engine for pattern matching'. For Chomsky, human language is of a different kind to that of an AI. It is tethered to a real world, and is socially focused. It understands impossibility, negative spaces and structural dependencies. It comes from a person with values and beliefs.

The problem, though, is that the examples Chomsky gave in March 2023 where 'machines can't do this' actually *could* be done, even at the time he wrote that piece. Today, they're twice as good. Even if Chomsky might be right that our 'universal grammar' still puts us ahead, it's likely only a matter of time before LLMs can beat it.

Kahneman
The Dark Side of Efficiency

If you ever think you've had a hard day, imagine what it's like to be a brain. Every day, your brain orchestrates a symphony of cognitive activities: analysing sensory input, crafting thoughts, calculating decisions and expressing emotions. It juggles conscious tasks with unconscious processes; it's reading this sentence while keeping your heart beating. The brain stores and retrieves memories, learns new skills and navigates the complexities of human relationships, all within a constantly changing external environment. Yes, it's not easy to be a brain.

So, who can blame it for taking a few shortcuts once in a while? When you're keeping an apex species alive, you need to do whatever you can to get by. These shortcuts might sometimes be automatic, like your brain's selective attention. For example, you can always see your nose, but your brain ignores it. It's got bigger fish to fry.

But, according to the Israeli-American psychologist Daniel Kahneman, when it comes to decision-making, your brain employs quick-fix strategies known as heuristics. These are tricks that your mind uses to make it easier for you to make a decision. And in the red-toothed wilderness of pre-modernity, being able to make a quick decision could save your life. But these heuristics can often lead to systematic errors. They make us blind to reason and utterly incapable of seeing things logically.

A great example of this is the representativeness heuristic, a bias which leads us to stereotype and make sweeping generalisations. On the face of it, stereotyping sounds like something which is always bad. But you do it all the time. If I asked you to get me some eggs, would you go to the library or the supermarket? Your company is about to launch a new jewellery product; do you target men or women more? You need some help with your computer; do you ask your young nephew or your elderly grandfather?

In each case, we've applied a heuristic, and it normally works for us. But of course, there's a shadowy side to heuristics we call 'biases'. This is when a teacher has higher expectations of a girl than a boy. It's when a boss promotes someone wearing a good suit and who talks in a posh voice. It's when police officers stop and search black people more than white people. Being alert to the biases in ourselves and others is important for any psychology student.

Kahneman and his long-term collaborator Amos Tversky introduced us to the concept of cognitive bias, a concept that is fairly mainstream and widespread these days. We are all much more aware of the fact that we are not hyper-logical robots. We do not see the world objectively, or like some unfiltered movie reel. How we think and what we think about are filtered through both our socialisation and biological necessity. You are not entirely rational; you're human.

Everyday Psychology
Singing to Your Baby

Peter is driving along his dreary, dull commute. He's dimly aware of the world, and his mind is sifting through the day ahead. Then, flowing from the radio directly into his *being*, comes the gentle deepness of Elgar's cello concerto. The drive is forgotten. Peter becomes immersed in the adagio – lifted away and into … what?

Most of us can relate to Peter's experience. If not Elgar, it might be a painting, a poem, a book, a building or a movie, something that throws us out of the normal way of doing things and into a different state altogether – a trance-like, meditative and quasi-spiritual state.

We know that music does us a lot of good. From many studies across multiple countries we know that music reduces anxiety, makes you more efficient at certain tasks and makes you sleep better. One of the more direct and powerful effects of music is on memory and learning. There's the so-called 'Mozart effect', where listening to certain types of music can make you focus better and retain facts easier. But there's also the role music plays in eliciting memory. Have you ever heard a song on the radio and been instantly reminded of a certain person, a certain time or a certain experience? Well, that's pretty common. Music is so good at nudging our recollection that it's often used for patients with dementia, where it can restore memories, even if only temporarily.

The deeper question, though, is *why* music has all these positive effects. With something like taking a walk outside, we can perhaps point to some underlying evolutionary mechanism to explain its benefits. But, with the possible exception of singing, music is not found in nature. And so we're left with best guesses and pseudoscience. Arthur Schopenhauer, for example, argued that music was a mystical gateway to some underlying truth – a melodic mirror to 'the Will'. And, while it *might* be true that percussion reminds us of a womb state and our mother's heartbeat, we really don't know why music helps us so much.

What we do know is that music is found in all human societies. It's thought that as soon as we could use our voices at all, we used them to make music. When a parent sings to their child, it facilitates bonding through the release of oxytocin and β-endorphin. When we listen to a song's lyrics alongside a melancholic or lilting melody, we're often overwhelmed by intense feelings that are much stronger than if we were to simply read those words. Music touches aspects of our being that words and noise cannot. It's psychology, but it feels like more.

Festinger
Why You're Never Wrong About Anything

Grant campaigned for a certain political party at the last general election. He's a card-carrying member and has donated his fair share to the party over the years. He went door to door with leaflets, telling everyone about the prosperous idyll the country would become if his party won. His party did win, and Grant partied hard. But over the following years, it became obvious that the government was awful. The prime minister was betraying all their key pledges, and the country was, by almost every metric, worse off.

Grant now has two things straining in his head. First, there is the fact that he devoted a portion of his life and wallet to this party. Second, there is the fact that the party has turned out to be rubbish. Two conflicting beliefs. Surely Grant couldn't have wasted so much on a party that was awful? And so, to save face and preserve some kind of consistency, Grant has to get rid of one of these beliefs. He can either downplay his involvement and the amount of time he invested or he has to ignore how rubbish the party is: 'Actually, they've done a lot of good for retired men in north Cornwall.'

This is known as cognitive dissonance theory, and the idea goes back to the American social psychologist Leon Festinger.

Festinger suggested that humans do not like holding two contradictory beliefs at the same time. We all like to imagine ourselves as logical, consistent and sensible people, so the presence of cognitive dissonance causes us great discomfort. To ameliorate this, we try to change or dilute the conflicting beliefs. Another example: suppose you spent a month researching smartphones and finally bought one. It's expensive, but oh so cool. Then you start to notice small things that annoy you: it's too large to hold easily, the camera is a bit slow and the battery is pretty bad. But because you've spent so much money and effort, you ignore these problems. You pretend they're not problems at all: 'It's fine, I'll just charge it twice a day,' or, 'I only ever use it with two hands anyway.' The discomfort of having chosen badly is alleviated.

Cognitive dissonance explains a lot of human behaviours. It explains why some people are hugely resistant to change – because to change implies that you made the wrong decision before. It might even account for why some people refuse to get help or therapy. When you admit you need help, then you're forced to recognise that something is wrong with your beliefs or behaviours.

It's hard to recognise our own cognitive-dissonance behaviours. No one likes to look stupid, and no one wants to think they've made a mistake. To preserve our self-respect and self-image, we will often perform great acts of mental gymnastics to *pretend* everything is fine.

Tulving

A Walk Down Memory Lane

Psychologists don't daydream, they enter a state of 'autonoetic consciousness'. Autonoetic consciousness is like taking a holiday in your mind. You start out thinking about that man at work with an odd beard. Then, your mind drifts into an associated memory – your last hairdressing appointment, perhaps. Next appears that girl you once dated at school, the one with the strange, off-red hair. Whatever happened to her? Didn't her mum die when she was sixteen? Now, you're at your uncle's funeral from last year. Your autonoetic holiday has taken a sombre turn.

When we pull back from our autonoetic walk down memory lane, we should take a moment to think of the Canadian psychologist Endel Tulving, who coined the term 'autonoetic'.

In the 1970s, Tulving released a series of papers that made an important distinction between 'semantic' and 'episodic' memory. Episodic memory is made up of episodes from your past, and recalling them is an act of mental time travel. Picture your first kiss. That's episodic memory. Semantic memory, on the other hand, is trivia. It's the dates, names and details. It's remembering *the name* of your first kiss.

The other interesting concept Tulving (with Donald Thomson) gave us is the 'encoding specificity principle' – a cumbersome name that is, ironically, very hard to retain. This is the idea that if you are trying to remember something from your past (you're trying to jumpstart your episodic memory), you'll have greater success if you place yourself in a similar situation to the one where you first established that memory.

For example, let's say you witnessed a car crash and you're called to the police station to give testimony. 'Do you remember if the light was red or green?' the police officer says. You have no idea. A few days later, you are driving by the same spot and suddenly you *can* remember. It was red. Being in the same space triggered the memory.

The encoding specificity principle is a proven and underappreciated aspect of memory. If you want to do well in an exam, try to revise in conditions similar to those in the exam hall. And it's also true for moods. If you go to a place that makes you relaxed – a favourite coffee shop, perhaps – you will feel relaxed. Likewise, if you go back to your family home at Christmas, you might find yourself feeling tetchy, claustrophobic and behaving like a child.

Tulving's episodic vs. semantic memory revisits an important point about our minds more broadly (see Gardner, pages 182–3). When people say, 'I've got a rubbish memory,' they are often referring to semantic memory. For them, school might have been a nightmare parade of poor marks and being told they're stupid. Semantic memory does not define intelligence, and it is only a subset of our wider memory systems. It just happens to be the one we grade students on.

Piaget
Daring to Talk to Children

Occasionally, a new parent will give me their baby to hold. I'll jiggle, coo and do all the things you're meant to. But then I throw in a curveball.

'Babies are okay, but they're basically like plants, aren't they?'

A pause. A crossroads. Either the parent will laugh and agree or they'll take deep offence at the fact that I've just compared sweet, darling baby James to a cactus. In this case, I'll turn to Piaget for help.

'Oh, I meant in developmental terms. According to the twentieth-century Swiss developmental psychologist Jean Piaget, in the first sensorimotor stages of life, a baby is basically reactive. They're slaves to sensory input. Of course I didn't mean James photosynthesises!'

Now you, too, can use Piaget to insult your friends' babies.

In my earlier book *Mini Philosophy*, I explore Piaget's theory of cognitive development because, although he's certainly a psychologist, his work has huge philosophical implications. Piaget argued that we move from the sensorimotor/plant stage into a preoperational stage (two to seven years old), where we develop abstract concepts and symbolic thoughts. Then, as we move through the operational stage (seven to eleven years), we develop the ability to think logically, before the formal operational stage (eleven years and up) opens up abstract, hypothetical and deductive reasoning. In other words, our minds are not born to us. Everything about the way we think grows as we do. And it grows in a specific environment.

What makes Piaget stand out in the history of psychology is his research. Up until Piaget's clinical work, psychology was not far from philosophy, the abstract reflections of theorists who rarely interacted with real people. Developmental psychology, if it could even be identified as such, hadn't moved much along since the seventeenth-century philosopher John Locke. Children were treated as having adult minds with adult cognitive processes. The difference between a parent and a toddler was simply exposure to the world. Children just needed to learn more things.

Piaget observed hundreds of children playing and learning at different stages of life. How the academic community of the time must have laughed as Piaget interviewed children. Talking to kids! Whatever next? In fact, Piaget was so concerned with his experiments that he veered close to obsession. Over his life, he wrote over 120,000 pages of research notes. One of his researchers once said, 'He is like a lion who roars for data.' He'd wake his researchers up at midnight, asking them to do this and that experiment. Rigorous, determined and thorough – but not someone you'd necessarily want as a boss.

Piaget's legacy is not only in his theories, which still form the backbone of modern developmental psychology, but also in his approach to the discipline. He recognised that speculation was not enough. Psychology needed to be a science.

Everyday Psychology
The Flow State

Akio sits on a wooden stool, hunched over his bonsai tree, his eyes fixed. He has been sitting there for three hours and he hasn't noticed the time. The vast busyness of the world has shrunk to the tiny tree before him. Every few minutes, he will lift a leaf, inspect its tiny veins, then move on to the next. Only twice, so far, has Akio made a cut with his sheers, and each time it is a gentle ten-minute labour. Akio's aching back is crying out for attention, but time itself bows to this moment of bonsai care.

Akio exemplifies the 'flow state'.

In 1975, the Hungarian psychologist Mihaly Csikszentmihalyi was fascinated by certain artists he knew who would sit for days at a time in one place to create their art. It was something so alien to most people's day-to-day bustle that he wanted to understand it. And so Csikszentmihalyi coined the term 'flow', like the flow of a river drifting along its course.

A flow state is any moment where you immerse yourself so fully in a single act that everything else seems to vanish. It might be an afternoon watching birds in the park or when an hour spent colouring goes by in a blink. Your entire attention is fixated on the task at hand. From his interviews with artists, Csikszentmihalyi identified various aspects of a flow state, but there are two essential ones.

First, the activity is seen as valuable. Akio is fixated on his tree, and the process of trimming, inspecting and caring for it is seen as an end in itself. It's not for some competition; it's not to impress his friends; it's not to sell online. The art of bonsai is its own pleasure, and it makes him happy. If you sit on the sofa for hours utterly captivated by a novel, that's the flow state. If you read a textbook to get knowledge to pass an exam, it's not – that's utilitarian and instrumental.

Second, is the warping of time. Everyone knows that time can often feel relative. Three hours watching a movie is different from three hours of Auntie Lorna telling you about her cruise-ship holiday. But when you're in a flow state, time changes. Sometimes it might melt away, as in an afternoon spent playing the piano; at other times, it might slow down so that every second feels weighted with significance, as when a footballer is about to take a penalty kick.

Flow state is a phenomenological experience. It's a 'how it feels' report by people who've known what it's like. But there have been various studies investigating the effect. It's known to improve creativity in artists, productivity in students and success in sports. When was the last time you experienced a flow state?

Piaget
Red Flags Are Not Red Flags

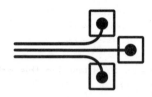

Freya is in a new relationship. She's been on a few dates; it's going well, and she's thinking of making it exclusive. But then she starts seeing red flags. He doesn't reply to messages quickly enough, he's got a lot of female friends, and he sometimes uses his phone in private. Of course, these aren't red flags; they're *Freya's* red flags. And they're down to Freya's *schema* for relationships – one of jealousy, suspicion and distrust.

Ian and Rachel have been together a few months; they're in love. One day, Ian notices something odd. Rachel gets changed weirdly. She puts on her *entire top half* first. She'll put on a shirt, jumper, jacket and so on first, and only then put on her underpants, trousers, etc. Ian is more disturbed than he ought to be, but he loves Rachel even more. Rachel has a *schema* for getting dressed.

The term 'schema' is a Greek word for the figure of a thing – a bit like a structure or a scaffold. Aristotle and the Stoics' work on propositional logic are early instances of schema-like concepts – they argued that all human reason depends on certain axioms or accepted starting points. They suggested that there are certain *structures* to our reasoning. A few millennia later, Immanuel Kant argued that we all have certain 'transcendental apperceptions'. These are the necessary conditions that allow us to have a mind at all. For instance, we have to have a sense of space to perceive objects.

But the idea of schema as we know it comes mostly from psychology. The Swiss psychologist Jean Piaget introduced the concept of schemas in cognitive development, suggesting that children construct and adjust their schemas through interaction with the environment. We have a model for how to interact with the world, and that model gets tinkered with and calibrated as we go on. In our opening stories, Freya and Rachel both have their schemas, which will either resist change ('Actually, Ian, this is the right way to do it!') or adapt to the evidence ('Oh, not *all* men are cheating scumbags').

Schemas are now seen as cognitive frameworks that help us organise and interpret information, affecting our attention and the encoding and retrieval of memories. They enable us to predict and interpret the world around us, but they can also lead to biases and misconceptions when information doesn't fit existing schemas. Prejudices of all kinds are built on schemas.

The difficulty with schemas is that it's desperately difficult – if not impossible, at times – to identify your own. We're all so tied up in our perceptions that when we just go about interacting with the world, we can't see our *method* of interacting with the world. I'm too busy looking at the sunrise to notice the rim of my glasses.

Neisser

The Problem with Psychology

If I ask you to add three and five together, what happens in your head? *How* do you add?

Remember the last time you went on a train. Remember where you sat, who you were with and where you were going. What's going on in your mind to *do* the remembering?

When a friend of yours walks into the room, how do you know that's your friend? What mental processes are going on?

The problem with psychology is that it's really hard to talk about a lot of it. When we consider our cognitive processes (like those above – arithmetic, memory, facial recognition and so on), we all know what it's like to use them, but it's hard for scientists to measure that. This meant that psychology for many decades was defined and dominated by 'behaviourism' (see pages 278-9).

Early psychologists were keen to establish the discipline very clearly as a science. It had to involve biological diagnoses, control groups and rigorous experimentation. It should present hypotheses to confirm or reject. But, as Ulric Neisser – the 'father of cognitive psychology' – recognised, this reduces psychology. It misrepresents what it is. If we are to study the mind, we also have to talk about those things that happen inside the head. We have to talk about internal mental states.

In 1967, Neisser criticised the existing psychology of his day in two ways. First, he challenged behaviourists' assumption that all human motivation and psychology could be explained by external factors. Second, he was dismissive of how artificial and abstracted the discipline had become. In an attempt to make a rigorous science of psychology, psychologists had conducted experiments in laboratories and in closed, fabricated conditions. But this is not what it is to actually live life.

Neisser's version of cognitive psychology said that we should look far more at the internal processes and experiences of having a mind. And, relatedly, we ought to consider the 'ecological validity' of the discipline – which is to say, how psychology can be studied and applied in everyday, practical and natural settings.

The problem that Neisser pointed out was that psychology occupies a strange place in the academic roster. On the one hand, it is, and needs to be, a science. It needs to hold itself to the strict rules of the scientific method. On the other hand, psychology walks remarkably close to the humanities. It's about internal mental processes and self-reporting. In fact, there's a perpetual, navel-gazing worry that psychology suffers from a replication crisis (see page 133) because of just how subjective and variable it is.

The fact is that psychology is a complex discipline because humans are complex and messy. We all present a sample size of one, and the only access any white-coated technician has to our mind is how we communicate it.

Sternberg
Adapting to the World

Robert liked school so far. He loved learning about the Egyptians in history, volcanoes in geography and planets in physics. But most of all he loved biology. He drew childish anatomical drawings at home and read about birds before bed. Then, one day, a psychologist came to school.

'Okay, kids,' he said, 'today we're going to do a special intelligence test.'

Robert clammed up. The psychologist scared him, and when he gripped his pencil, he saw his hand shaking. An hour later, he handed back his paper. Robert was declared an idiot. He scored poorly, so he was a dunce. Suddenly, he hated school. He didn't care about stupid Egyptians, and planets were for losers. He threw away his biology books. But Mrs Smith took him aside one day.

'Robert,' she said, holding his gaze. 'Listen to me. I don't care about those numbers. That test was bunk. I know you are one of the most brilliant and intelligent boys I've ever taught.'

This is the true story of Robert J. Sternberg, whose triarchic theory of intelligence ripped apart the idea that IQ meant intelligence.

Even today, nearly fifty years after Sternberg, we falsely equate 'book smarts' or IQ tests with intelligence. We assume that if someone is good at tests, can recite some poem or remembers a certain fact, they're intelligent. But Sternberg argued that true intelligence is not about trivia or academia, it's about adaptation. As he wrote in 1985: 'Intelligence is the mental activity directed towards purposive adaptation to selection and shaping of real-world environments relevant to one's life.'

Stenberg proposed that intelligence comprises three parts: analytical intelligence (problem-solving skills), creative intelligence (the ability to deal with new situations using past experiences and current skills) and practical intelligence (the ability to adapt to a changing environment).

Let's imagine a scenario. Three candidates apply for the same job at the Foreign Office. They've all got top degrees from top universities, and they've scrubbed up well for the occasion. They are each given a mock scenario where they have to respond to some 'live' event – a terrorist attack or something. Two candidates struggle and stutter. They've never come across this situation at university, so they freeze in the headlights. The third candidate ducks and weaves. They see commonalities and patterns. They ignore this bit and focus on that. They adapt. For Sternberg, this candidate is the most intelligent.

Today, intelligence is seen as so complicated that few reputable psychologists put a number on the 'types'. But Sternberg was part of a tradition that called out the nonsense that anyone is 'stupid'.

Sperling

How Much of This Book Will You Remember?

Readers of a certain age will remember *The Generation Game*. After several rounds of inter-generational family gaming, contestants had to face the conveyor belt. A series of twenty random and unrelated prizes rolled past them and they had to remember as many as they could to win them. The fun part was playing along at home.

Different people will have different qualities of memory but there's a strange thing that happens when you play the conveyor belt memory test. You try your hardest to remember the objects but you can *feel* them disappearing from your memory. It's as if the earlier or less memorable ones literally dissolve from your mental workstation. And, at the end of the show, when the chirpy host asks how you did, you can barely remember even the cuddly toy that comes up every week.

The Generation Game is just one example of what George Sperling proved in his experiments on memory, retention and processing.

In 1960, Sperling had participants look at a three-by-three grid of nine letters for a brief moment – no more than a blink of an eye. Afterwards, everyone had to write down as many characters as they could in what's called a 'whole-report' recall. On average, people could record four to five characters, but, more importantly, almost everyone said that they could remember seeing more but that they disappeared and existed just out of reach. They knew something was there, but it lay hidden behind the fog of memory.

To try and investigate if this were true, Sperling then performed a 'partial-report' experiment. Here he had participants look at the same grid, but this time he gave out a musical note to ask them to recall a specific row, for instance, a low tone for the lowest row. Oddly, almost all the participants could recall almost all of the letters in this way, suggesting they did, in fact, retain the entire grid.

Sperling's experiments led him to make the distinction between different types of memory stores: sensory, short-term and long-term memory. When we first see something, we form a near-perfect and complete image of that scene. This is known as an iconic memory. It's like a one-second photo shot. Sadly, for most of us, that image will fade within moments – but not all of it. Your memory system will pull out and retain the bits it deems to be the most relevant and interesting. That might be a lot. It might be hardly anything. This small part then gets passed on to your short-term memory system. Even here, though, the longevity of your brief experience is not guaranteed.

That evening, as you sleep, your memory systems are getting out their energy-efficient, space-making scalpel. Only the absolutely necessary will be retained. The rest will be flushed away as useless junk, never to be recalled again.

Everyday Psychology
Learn a Language

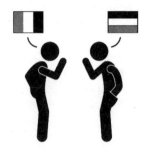

Bilingual people are incredibly attractive. If you don't agree with that, I'm afraid you're in the minority. In a 2018 survey of users on dating sites, 75 per cent of respondents said they were more likely to swipe yes for those who could speak multiple languages. But multilingualism isn't just good for your love life, it comes with a whole host of benefits. There is a growing body of research focused on the psychological, economic and health advantages of being bilingual. It improves a host of cognitive functions across all stages of life, and it affects our emotional and social attitudes as well.

Here are four ways speaking another language can improve your mind:

1. It improves multitasking. If you are speaking your non-native language, then you're constantly switching, shifting and processing different languages in real time. In 2011, Ellen Bialystok proved that bilinguals are better at non-linguistic multitasking as well. Their brains are better at hopping around.

2. It wards off Alzheimer's disease. As we get older, our cognitive functions will start winding down. With grey hair comes a loss of essential grey matter in the brain. At its worst, this will manifest itself as dementia, of which Alzheimer's is the most common form. In 2020, John Anderson et al. performed a huge meta-study and concluded that learning another language both reduces your chances of getting dementia and slows its progress if you do.

3. It makes you more empathetic. In 2018 study, Scott R. Schroeder concluded: 'Acquiring two languages helps theory of mind development [which is] the ability to attribute mental states to other people and to predict and explain other people's behaviour on the basis of those attributed mental states.' In other words, bilingualism allows people to adopt a 'meta-linguistic' position more easily. They can adopt not only another language but also another person's belief system.

4. It improves certain cognitive functions. All those little jobs your brain does without any praise whatsoever are called executive functions. If you scratched your ear while reading this sentence, that's an executive function. If you decide to read this sentence backwards, that's an executive function. Bilinguals are better at flipping between them. For example, in a 'Stroop test', bilinguals perform much better than monolinguals at differentiating visual (colours) and semantic (the meanings of words) confusions.

Although this entry sounds as if it were sponsored by Duolingo, the study of bilingualism reinforces a point made elsewhere in this book (pages 161 and 287). Your brain is a tool that rises to the job when you challenge it but will shrivel on the sofa if you don't. It's a muscle to bulk or atrophy, depending on how regularly you work out. And learning languages is one of the best ways to keep your mind sharp.

Kahneman
Leeeeroy Jenkins!

In the innocent internet days of 2005, a video about Leeroy Jenkins went viral. It showed a team preparing to enter a World of Warcraft dungeon. The group was plotting which weapons to use, which routes to take and what tactics to adopt. The kind of planning that put Omaha Beach to shame. Just as they were about to start, one of the players, who had been away eating chicken, came back and stormed into the dungeon, shouting, 'Leeeeroy Jenkins!' The horrified group ran in after Leeroy, but the damage was done. They were defeated. And Leeroy was immortalised in meme history.

Leeroy Jenkins embodies a certain type of person but also a certain type of thinking, and he can help us understand Daniel Kahneman's 'dual process' theory of cognition.

Plato argued that the human mind (psyche) is influenced by three competing forces: our instincts, our passions and our rationality. Rationality has to try to keep the other two in check. Two millennia later, William James argued that we have 'associative thinking' – mental habits or heuristics, the way we've learned to think – and then 'true reasoning', which is effortful reflection.

So, the idea of two ways of reasoning has been around for a while, but Kahneman's 2011 book *Thinking, Fast and Slow* brought it to widespread attention. Kahneman argued that all our decisions are run by two 'systems'. System 1 is our fast, intuitive and emotional thinking. It's the impulsive Leeroy Jenkins storming in. Then, there's System 2, which is our slower, more deliberative, logical thinking. It's the group deep in planning while Leeroy was eating chicken.

There is a time and a place for both. Most of the day, our brain operates on System 1: we eat when we're hungry, we recognise a face that we know and we drive our commute thoughtlessly. Instant, effortless and automatic. System 2 is for bigger issues but also kicks in to correct System 1. If a road is closed on your familiar route, System 2 takes over. When you meet someone new, you might have a first impression of them (System 1), which gradually changes after collecting evidence (System 2).

Kahneman's dual process theory is a useful way to understand certain mental health conditions. Anxiety, depression and obsession can often be caused by System 1 thinking that does not recalibrate to System 2 corrections. 'You've got nothing to be worried about!' usually won't work to resolve someone's anxiety because this System 2 reasoning can't dent their System 1.

Leeroy's charge and Kahneman's theory underline the tension between instinct and analysis, spontaneity and deliberation. Kahneman's framework offers not just an insight into our daily decisions but a lens through which to view the broader range of human behaviour. It reminds us that to conquer the dungeons of life we must balance our convictions with the wisdom of our reflections.

Gibson

Can You Eat Your Brother?

Look around you. Look at any of the objects you can see.

As you do, you will be presented with a series of 'optic arrays'. These are the patterns of light that hit your eye to inform you about the world. As you move your head and scan the area, the optic arrays change but they're still informing you about the shape, size and layout of what's in front of you.

Let's imagine that your optic array presents you with a horizontal, flat, extended and rigid surface. You see all the raw characteristics of a substance. But that's not all you see. You see a *table*. You see a surface that you can put things on, eat your dinner off and possibly sit on if you meet the requisite weight requirements.

According to the American psychologist James J. Gibson, the flat, rigid surface *affords* you support and tableness. This idea of affordability is essential to Gibson's 'ecological' approach to perception.

When you interact with the world, you are not making inferences. You do not see a long plastic item and deduce that it's pen. You do not look at a nose, an eye, a mouth and some hair and have to furrow your brow to conclude that's a face. When we perceive the world, we *immediately* and *directly* see things as they relate to us. We attach to our optic arrays an 'affordability' and ask, 'What can I use this thing for?' or 'What is it good for?'

For Gibson, affordances are opportunities for action. As Gibson puts it, the world does not just consist of abstract physical properties but has 'to be measured compared to the animal. It is unique for the animal [and] an affordance cannot be measured as we measure in physics ... The affordances of the environment are what it offers the animal, what it provides or furnishes, either for good or ill.'

When we encounter anything in the world, we measure it according to our needs and expectations. *Objects* can be used for whatever end we need, but when we meet other *animals*, we have a distinct set of affordances altogether. These affordances are as varied as we are, but Gibson suggests a few: sexual (can I have sex with this?), predatory (can I eat or be eaten by it?), nurturing (should I look after this?), fighting (is this a danger?), playing (can I enjoy this?), cooperating (should I help or get help from this?) and communication (can I talk to this?).

So, when you next look around you, try to think about both how strange and easily familiar your affordances are. Is a tree to be enjoyed, climbed or cut down for wood? When you next see your sibling, are they going to help you or will they eat you?

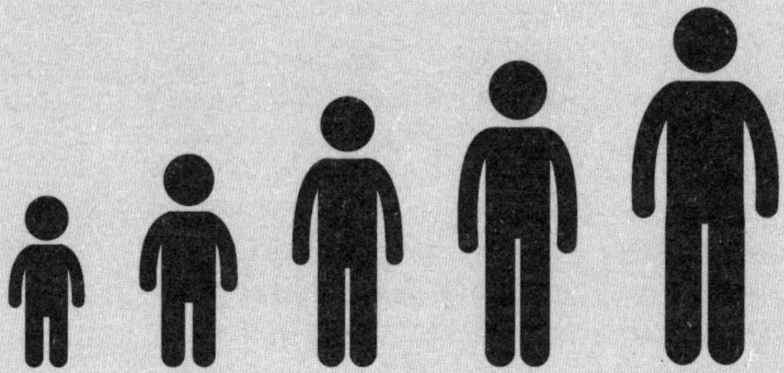

Developmental Psychology

It's a strange fact of human nature that you never really feel yourself growing up. It just happens. One day, you were a short, naïve child who could touch their toes. Now, you've seen the world, read some books and your joints ache in the cold. Developmental psychology is what tracks that journey. It looks at the ages and stages of mental progress and where it can go wrong.

Developmental psychology is about how our minds grow from childhood to adulthood.

Pinker
A Debate Worth Having

The nature vs. nurture debate is one of the oldest in history. How much of your personality is a product of your environment and upbringing, and how much is due to your innate mental and physiological wiring? It's simultaneously one of the most vitriolic debates you can have and one of the most enjoyable. Consider these questions:

Is your sexuality made by your environment or born to you?

Is addiction more down to our biology or our upbringing?

Are aggression, empathy, cowardice, extroversion, depression or narcissism the result of 'nature' or 'nurture'?

Most reputable writers have recognised that a human mind is never entirely the product of one or the other, though most lean towards one side. But, according to the American cognitive psychologist Steven Pinker, for the last few decades we have been pushing nature aside. The existing academic paradigm is all about our environment – we're entirely made a certain way, never born like that. It's a paradigm that Pinker aims to break.

In his book *The Language Instinct*, Pinker suggests that humans are born with a built-in capacity for language – a belief he and Chomsky have in common (pages 52–3). And if this one major component of human cognition is innate, it makes sense to at least consider that others are too. Pinker goes on to argue that there is a strong genetic component to human behaviour and thinking patterns, suggesting that many aspects of the mind are innately *structured* rather than solely shaped by the environment.

If we pause to consider, Pinker says, we'll see 'there are a number of reasons to doubt that the human mind is a blank slate. [For example,] anyone who's had more than one child knows that kids come into the world with certain temperaments and talents.' Humans have roughly just under 50,000 genes. Genes are designed to code proteins to make the body behave a certain way. Sometimes, that's about scabbing over a cut; other times, though, it's neural. Genes encode how you think.

Pinker believes there are two 'political reasons' behind the rejection of our 'nature'. First, if we accept that some people are born a certain way, that undermines the idea of equality. Some people are literally better than others at certain things. Some people are *born* smarter, faster, stronger, healthier and more attractive than others. The worry is that this leads to discrimination. The second reason is the fear is that focusing on genetics will lead to *eu*genics – the idea that we can selectively breed a better humanity.

However sound these reasons might be, they deny the science: humans are neither fully influenced by nurture or by nature. Yes, we might not be blank slates, but neither are we robots, acting as slaves to our genetic instructions. Pinker doesn't solve the nature vs. nurture debate. He simply restates that it's a debate worth having.

Kohlberg
I *Am* the Law!

Has your sense of right and wrong changed over the years? Are there things you see as acceptable today that you'd have found outrageous when you were younger? If you spend time around children, you might notice how starkly different their sense of morality is. You will notice how black and white, egocentric or oddly rational it can be.

These are questions Lawrence Kohlberg asked, and his idea of the 'stages of moral development' dominates moral psychology today.

Kohlberg gave roughly sixty children of different ages a series of moral dilemmas. They were offered open-ended questions to explain their answers. For instance, in one dilemma, 'Heinz' needs an expensive drug for his dying wife. He can't afford it, so he has to steal it. Should he: (a) not steal it because that's breaking the law; (b) steal it and go to jail for breaking the law; or (c) steal it but be let off because it's unfair?

If you have young children in your life, try it on them. '*Mini Psychology*: Encouraging Child Experimentation.'

From the answers he received, Kohlberg identified three stages of our moral development:

1. *Pre-conventional*: This is an egocentric hedonism that wants only to avoid punishment or claim reward. 'Good' means what's beneficial to oneself, and 'bad' is what's negative. Ultimately, a kid doesn't want to go to their room or the naughty step, and they do want ice cream. So they act nice and get the good stuff.

2. *Conventional*: This reflects a growing sense of social belonging and is other-regarding. Approval and praise are seen as rewards, and behaviour is calibrated to please others, obey the law and promote the good of the family, tribe or nation. It focuses on obeying the rules, but more from a desire to be *seen* as good. This maps well onto answer a) above.

3. *Post-conventional*: This challenges authority and involves an element of self-reflection and moral reasoning. It involves a belief that certain principles are above fixed laws, such as justice or fairness. Laws, or 'rules', are not themselves moral but need to exist alongside bigger principles. Answers b) and c) could, in different ways, reflect this kind of moral flexibility.

Kohlberg identified these stages as a developmental progression from early infancy all the way to adulthood, but it might be that some people never progress at all. We may know people who are resolutely bound to the conventional stage or even the egocentric stage (which is associated with psychopathy).

So, what's your answer to the Heinz dilemma? Where do you fall on Kohlberg's scale? And is he right to view it as a hierarchical maturation, or might we become more immoral as we get older?

Vygotsky
It's Good to Talk

We thrive by talking. It's by talking that we run up against other human minds, and this *always* has implications. The moment we learn to speak, everything changes. Suddenly, we can tell people our thoughts and demand things from them. Most importantly, we can ask questions. To a young child, everyone is a teacher, and, for better or worse, the people surrounding that child will form the cultural and social background that'll build their mind. Talking is the tool by which we develop; it defines how we act and how we think.

This was how the Soviet psychologist Lev Vygotsky saw the human mind. He showed that we learn by interacting with others.

For Vygotsky, we are not isolated autodidactic geniuses with a bounty of innate ideas within us. Instead, we develop by engaging with others in the form of 'cultural activities'. These are the things we share with each other, like language, number systems, societal values and so on. But, most often, it's simply about how we talk to others.

When we learn to talk with other people, we don't just open a conversation, we open the door on an education. When a child speaks to an adult (or other children), they learn a certain grammatical system, but they also learn *what* to talk about and *how*. It's through conversations that we develop that inner voice in our heads which then guides and structures our worldview. It builds our schema (see pages 66–7). Our entire mental life is shaped by who we talk to and what we talk about. For instance, if your family is constantly negative, gossiping and sniping, then you'll learn that is the 'normal' way to approach the world. Or if a child's friends are always talking about body image, they'll find themselves thinking about it too. The voices we hear and the answers we get change us. As Vygotsky said: 'Through others, we become ourselves.'

This has huge implications for educational psychology. Since children's minds are created by our interactions, our teachers take on magnified importance. This led to one of Vygotsky's key insights: the 'zone of proximal development' (ZPD). The ZPD shows that if a child is working alongside a competent teacher, they can complete tasks far beyond their normal abilities. If a child (or anyone, actually) works with someone else, they can unlock potential they lack on their own. The ZPD describes how far a child could reach with help.

Talking does so much good. It lets us bond with each other, and it's often the best form of therapy (see page 31). More than that, though, it's what allows us to have thoughts at all. Vygotsky's lesson is that if we're made by the company we keep, we should really make sure we choose that company wisely.

Ainsworth
Learning What Love Means

If I ask you to imagine 'married life', what do you see? If I ask you to think of 'a healthy relationship', what do you picture? In both cases, your idea has been informed by the specific environment in which you grew up. We are all the product of the statistical inference that is childhood, and we learn everything about the world from our earliest interactions with other humans. If you had parents who always praised you and loved you unconditionally, then you will be confident and secure. If you had parents who barely interacted with you and who seemed to care more for the TV than you, then you will grow to become distant and anxious. A young child with unattached parents will learn unattachment.

This was exactly what concerned the developmental psychologist Mary Ainsworth in her version of attachment theory.

In the 1970s, Ainsworth was keen to build on John Bowlby's attachment theory (see pages 34–5). She developed the famous 'strange situation' test, in which a parent arrives with a child. They both interact with the toys they find. Then a stranger enters and attempts to play with the child. Then the parent exits the room, leaving the stranger alone with the child. Then the stranger exits, leaving the child entirely alone. Finally, of course, the parent returns.

Ainsworth observation of the children's behaviours led her to formalise three types of attachment styles:

- *Type A* people are insecure-avoidant and made up roughly 15 per cent of her study. These children are highly independent and seem oddly unconcerned by both the exit of their parent and the arrival of the stranger. They displayed no 'safe base' or 'proximity-seeking' behaviours like cuddling up or hiding behind a caregiver.

- *Type B* people are secure in their attachment and made up 70 per cent of the study. They were moderately and healthily anxious about the stranger and the caregiver's departure, but calmed down quickly when the parent was around.

- *Type C* people are ambivalent in their relationship with a caregiver, and these made up the last 15 per cent. These children didn't trust their parents to stay with them or look after them, so they clung desperately to them. They cried, screamed and struggled to be with the parent at all times.

While subsequent research has expanded these types and fleshed out their differences, the basic model Ainsworth proposed has been proven and proven again.

The sad truth behind Ainsworth's theory is that whenever you meet someone who's prickly, distant and rude, you're not meeting a hard person but a hard upbringing. Here is someone who could never trust their parents and had to fend for themselves early on. They grew up too quickly. These people never learned how to form proper, secure and meaningful relationships, because they never had one themselves.

Everyday Psychology
The Media Get It Wrong

One of the most common TV and movie tropes is the high-functioning, hyper-intelligent, case-cracking savant. It's in *Rain Man*, *Sherlock*, *House M.D.*, *Criminal Minds*, *Monk*, and so on. In each case, the audience is led to believe that there is some kind of underlying neural pathology at work, usually autism. Many of these representations of mental health conditions are done with the best intentions and, at least in recent years, normally come from a place of respect. But the entertainment industry has not always been good at representing neurodiverse characters.

In 2000, the Australian psychologist Anthony Jorm wrote a paper about mental health illiteracy. He concluded that the vast majority of the general public around the world is woefully ignorant about mental illness. There are two related reasons for this. The first is a lack of education. And so, often, the *only* exposure people get to these conditions is through popular culture. The vast majority of people are learning about mental health via the TV screen.

Unfortunately, the makers of TV programmes are not psychiatric experts, nor is that their job. Their job is entertainment, and accuracy is often the first casualty in the hunt for a watchable show. The portrayals of mental illness on TV or in the movies are often superficial and stigmatising. They exaggerate certain elements, such as violence, eccentricity or savantism, while downplaying the everyday struggles and realities of living with various conditions. For example, there is no substantive evidence to link most mental illnesses with aggression, and yet most people believe that those with neurological conditions are dangerous, unpredictable and violent. Representations of mental health are often either openly or subtly used for a laugh in a way that's demeaning and belittling. Most people learn about mental health from TV, and what they're learning is that these conditions are to be feared, shunned, laughed at or denigrated.

There are huge and damaging implications to this. It often reinforces a millennia-old stigma, keeping the neurodiverse at arm's reach. They're not in asylums any more, but they're still stigmatised. Which means that those with these conditions are ashamed, and those who believe they *might* have them will refuse to seek proper diagnosis and help. TV and movies rarely, if ever, show the actual treatment plan of someone living with a mental health condition. There might be a psychoanalytic scene, but little is ever shown about medication or behavioural therapy (see pages 16–17) because it's just not cinematically interesting.

Of course, things are getting better, both in terms of how well educated the public is about mental health and within the entertainment industry itself. But the next time you see someone with a mental health condition on screen, ask yourself whether it's a fair representation.

Bronfenbrenner
Who Holds the Chisel?

If you lived a century ago, you'd probably only care about what a hundred people or so think. Your family, your friends and probably a few people in your neighbourhood. That was it. You would wear certain clothes to fit in with those people. You'd use certain words to sound like them. You'd make major life decisions based on (or in rebellious reply to) those people.

Today, things are different. Suddenly, we don't care about a hundred people; we care about a million. We compare ourselves to celebrities on the other side of the planet and obsess over the 'likes' of strangers with anonymous usernames. We learn about different cultures and ways of doing things. Our language is as much another hemisphere's as it is our neighbourhood's.

In Urie Bronfenbrenner's phrase, we live in a different 'ecosystem'.

We are all made, to some extent, by our environments. We are the unformed clay that gets chiselled away by seen and unseen sculptors. But who holds the chisel? For Bronfenbrenner, we are all subject to a variety of different environmental pressures, which will exert more or less pressure depending on who we are.

For example, for most people, your most important ecosystem is still your 'microsystem' – your parents, school, work and neighbours. These are the people you see almost every day and for long periods of time. But we are also influenced by things like the media (exosystem), social norms (macrosystems) and even our point in world history (chronosystem). Bronfenbrenner's ecosystems act a little like a Maslow's pyramid (see pages 202–3) for child development. The microsystem is the most important to grounded and happy children, and if this breaks down (with abusive or absent parents, toxic friendships or sustained hardship), then it can lead to crippling mental health issues.

Bronfenbrenner knew that these systems are not self-contained; instead they are like Russian dolls hiding and being hidden in turn. Your identity is overwhelmingly influenced by your parents, but your parents were influenced by their siblings, who were influenced by the economic environment, which was defined by the socio-political zeitgeist. In some ways, we are passively influenced, as we cannot change social norms. In other ways, it's bi-relational, for instance, when we ditch a toxic friendship or change workplace.

Bronfenbrenner's theories mostly stemmed from his work on child development in the 1960s, but they could easily be applied to you and me in the here and now. Who do you think is the greatest influence on your life today? How much power do you have to move ecosystems or shuffle their contents? We might not be able to entirely make ourselves, but we can choose who we want to make us.

Bandura

We Are What We See

A young boy sits at a table, and he watches. He watches a lot. Sometimes he talks and listens, plays and fights, but he's always watching. Today, he's watching his uncle play the guitar. He's never heard the guitar before. He sits at the table, his eyes glazed in wonder, his jaw slack with concentration. He's entranced. The boy watches and he *learns*. He learns that it's acceptable to sing in public and that you can play an instrument with your family. He learns how to hold a guitar and what it looks like to strum and move your fingers. He learns what it feels like to hear someone play something that *moves* you.

A lot happens when we watch. According to the Canadian-American psychologist Albert Bandura, it's one of the most powerful and interesting ways we can learn anything.

When you acquire any new skill, you have to learn how to do it. There are two ways to do this. Either you do it yourself or you watch someone else do it. A good example of the former might be touch-typing. It's perfectly reasonable to expect someone new to computers to be given a keyboard and told, 'Good luck, off you go.' At first, they crawl along with intense, single-fingered concentration. But give it enough time, and that someone will develop the ability to type fluently and quickly, without ever being shown how.

According to Bandura, though, most of the skills we learn are through 'observational learning' – we see others do a thing and then try to do it ourselves. This need not even be real-life observation, either. Bandura found evidence to say that 'symbolic models' found in books or on TV can often teach us how to behave. But most of the time, observational learning is about watching the people in your life – parents, siblings, teachers or friends. We watch someone else do a thing, and we learn. Sadly, Bandura's own experiments in the 1960s were somewhat more depressing than the scenario of a young boy and his musical uncle. Bandura divided a group of seventy-two children aged between three and six into groups. One group watched an adult treat a 'Bobo doll' horribly. The adult would shout, attack and abuse the doll. The other group saw an adult treat the doll kindly, playing gently. As you would expect, the aggressive group learned to treat their dolls aggressively. The gentle group learned gentleness.

The reality is that children, all over the country, are watching their own versions of the Bobo doll. They're watching how Dad constantly mocks Mum. They're watching how their friends behave in class. They're watching how their symbolic models on social media talk and behave.

We aren't what we eat, we're what we see.

Harlow
Traumatised Monkeys

In 1958, American psychologist Harry Harlow did some controversial experiments on monkeys. He took a group of infant monkeys from their mothers at birth and put them into cages. He gave the monkeys two surrogate 'mothers'. The first 'mother' was a cold, lifeless wire model, but with food provision (a bottle of milk). The second surrogate was a lifelike, towel-covered monkey doll. Would the monkeys prefer wire and food or the cloth mother with no food? Well, monkeys aren't stupid. They went to the wire model when they were hungry. They knew where the food was coming from. But what Harlow noted was that for most of the day the monkeys would almost all stay near the towel mother. They would snuggle close to the doll and only go to the wire model when they needed food.

This led Harlow to conclude that monkeys – and, by extension, most primates – value comfort and tactile, emotional bonds over only sustenance.

In a second experiment, Harlow divided the monkeys into two groups. One group *only* had the wire with food surrogate, and the other group *only* had the cloth surrogate, but this time with food as well. Both groups grew at the same rate. But the group with the wire surrogate was deeply psychologically damaged. They were easily scared, reluctant to explore (see pages 34–5 on Bowlby), would not stand up for themselves, would find it hard to have sex, and made bad mothers.

While we have to be careful when extrapolating monkey data to humans, it seems reasonable to suggest that Harlow proved that we all need comfort and attachment. We need them more than sustenance. When we're forced into a life where we're denied these connections, it can cause great, lasting, scarring damage.

There's something deeply sad about Harlow's experiments – today they would certainly be deemed unethical. The baby monkeys would desperately try to get some love or attention from their wire surrogate mothers, nuzzling, hugging and jumping on the wire model. You can imagine how, after a few months of trying, the infant monkey would learn that it would not get any kind of meaningful affection. The monkey adapts. A bit of the monkey breaks.

It's sad because this is the story of so many people alive today. It's the story of a young child trying to play with a dad constantly on his smartphone. It's the story of a baby trying to cuddle a mother who's passed out from drug abuse on the sofa. It's about absent parents, abusive caregivers and loneliness. Harlow's experiments proved again that we all need to know that we're loved. We need much more than simply food and water if we're to grow up whole.

Merleau-Ponty
Seeing the Whole Picture

Look around you now, and what do you see? What you'll probably do is list all the objects in sight – a tree, a chair, a person, a cloud, a coffee cup and so on. But this is not how humans actually encounter the world. At every moment, we do not meet discrete objects but a tableau. We are not robots analysing individual things and trying to put them into some coherent order. We're immersed in a scene in which all the objects belong together. The tree next to the fence, the door framed by the wall, the clouds blotting a blue sky.

This is what Maurice Merleau-Ponty noted in his analysis of 'gestalt'.

Merleau-Ponty was equal parts psychologist and philosopher at a time when the two disciplines hated each other. In fact, he was chair of both the Child Psychology and Philosophy departments at the Sorbonne at different times. Merleau-Ponty contested the dominant view at the time (descended from John Locke) that our knowledge comes from our individual experiences of the world. Merleau-Ponty argued instead that we do not experience separate sensations, like 'yellow', 'oval' or 'waxy'; we simply perceive an already unified 'lemon'. We see the entire picture. We see the 'gestalt'.

Perception does not focus on this or that sensation. Rather, it is a 'spontaneous organisation of the sensual field', where 'each element is determined by its function in the whole'. No experiences are isolated; we're unavoidably bombarded with the totality of a scene.

An old Daoist philosopher, Zhuangzi, once wrote: 'A baby looks at things all day without squinting; that is because his eyes are not focused on any particular object ... He merges himself within the surroundings and moves along with them.' If you look at a baby, you'll notice they just stare at things. But they are not staring at this or that object; they are looking at the barrage of sensation that is everything. During our cognitive development, adult humans teach young humans to delineate, define and classify things. For Merleau-Ponty, deconstructing things into component sensations like this actually demands artificial effort. Your everyday lived experience does not take place in some abstract realm. We are interacting with the whole of things.

This is most true in how we view other people (and ourselves). For instance, if someone is angry, you don't focus on the details of the red face, clenched jaw or crossed arms. You just see anger.

Ancient Chinese wisdom and modern psychology can teach us a valuable lesson: do not try to deconstruct the world. Life cannot be fitted into neat boxes, and the universe cannot be reduced to labels. Take the world as it comes. See the bigger picture and recognise yourself as simply part of it all.

Baumrind
The Three Types of Parent

There are a lot of entries in this book which will keep me up at night. Most people know that parents are important, and that getting the best parenting makes the best kind of children become the best kind of adults. But, having spent the last few years with my nose deep in the knotty, overbearing world of psychoanalysis, I'm beginning to get nervous. I've got young children. They're like high-energy sponges looking to me for guidance, teaching and love. Every word I say has to be right. Every action must be carefully choreographed to ensure healthy, happy children. And so I've read a small library's worth of parenting books. My social media algorithm is forever skewed towards rainy-day activities with the kids.

Which is why I'm so annoyed that I've only now come across Diana Baumrind's 'parenting styles'. I'm doubly annoyed because Baumrind's research came out seventy-five years ago, and it's clearer and more honest than all the books I've read.

Baumrind started from the position of a confused, anxious parent. She knew that parenting is a complex interplay of parental expectations, disciplinary strategies, communication styles, cultural norms and nurturing behaviours. All shaken and stirred with sleep deprivation, endless winter sicknesses and nappies. But after years of research as a child and developmental psychologist, Baumrind isolated three different types of parenting styles.

1. *Authoritative* parents are supportive and take an interest in their kids' activities, but they are not overbearing. They allow children to make constructive (and safe) mistakes and encourage independent decision-making. Children who grow up in authoritative households tend to have higher self-esteem, better social skills and lower levels of depression compared to their peers.

2. *Authoritarian* parents are strict and have high expectations for their children's behaviour. They're the caricature of some shouty, ex-military dad or a priggish, sharp-tongued mum. They use punishment to enforce rules and often do not explain the reasoning behind their demands. Children raised in authoritarian environments are more likely to be obedient and proficient but score lower in happiness, social competence and self-esteem. They are high-achieving but troubled.

3. *Permissive* parents are lenient and rarely enforce rules or boundaries. They avoid confrontation and are more likely to act as friends to their children. They let the kids run amok – crayon on the walls and chocolate for breakfast. Children reared by permissive parents tend to rank low in happiness and self-regulation and will likely have problems with authority.

While it seems simplistic to reduce *all* parenting to three categories, Baumrind's styles leave huge scope for individual variations. It does not reduce parents to cookie-cutter labels but rather provides frameworks around which to add your own values.

Erikson

Pulled Every Which Way

There's an ancient Celtic poem called the 'Song of Amergin' about a druid who arrives on the coast of Ireland. It features twelve lines, each starting with the words 'I am' followed by a description.

I am the bull of seven battles.

I am the eagle on the rock.

I am a flash from the sun.

These are not the arrogant boasts of a chest-thumping bard. The poem is written to show that man cannot be reduced to one name alone. Each of the names represents an aspect of Amergin's nature: a stag for strength, the sea for depth, a boar for coarseness, and so on. Writing your own 'I am' poem of twelve lines is a great way to reflect on who you are. Find a quiet moment, alone and private, and give it a go.

But the problem with being a dodecagon is that it often leads to confusion. All of our many identities will not always gel. I am a partygoer, but I'm also a family man. I'm mischievous, but I'm also a rule-follower. There's tension in contradiction.

This is what led the twentieth-century psychoanalyst Erik Erikson (he had imaginative parents) to coin the term 'identity crisis'.

Erikson's theory of psychosocial development suggests that the story of life is a story of tensions. We are constantly pulled by different forces, and how we manage those conflicting forces determines how happy we are. Erikson suggests there are eight major conflicts over a lifetime. For example, when you're very young, there is a tension between trust and mistrust. You say, 'These people are my carers; let's trust them,' and, 'These people might be dangerous; let's avoid them.' Babies and toddlers need to establish the boundary between 'dangerous' and 'safe' to be happy. They need to find and join their own tribe. When you get to school, the tension is often between competence and inferiority. You're great at maths but crap at history. You learn that you cannot be a master of everything but oscillate between achievement and mediocrity.

For Erikson, one of the hardest conflicts to manage comes in adolescence, and this is where we find the 'identity crisis'. This is the tension between staying at home and going on an adventure. It's a conflict between the desire to be a loved child, with their clothes washed and food cooked, and the urge to be an independent adult and strike out into the world. Exploit or explore. Cuddle or struggle. Child or adult.

But Erikson's point was that we have identity crises all the time. Every 'I wish' about your life is a kind of mini-crisis. You might want to be more creative, take more risks and live in the fast lane. But you might also want a secure job, a comfortable home and a steady pay cheque. Everyone's crisis is different, but we all have one.

Sternberg
I Love You Like a Brother

In Sanskrit, there are ninety-six words for love. In Persian, there are eighty. Ancient Greek would look embarrassingly impoverished with its three words if it weren't for English: English has only one word for love. Of course, English has workarounds: we say 'brotherly' love, 'paternal' love, 'romantic' love, and so on. Most people agree that love is one of the greatest and most powerful feelings we can have, yet it's often very difficult to pin down. Consider this example.

Ben is married, and he loves his wife. But over a 24-hour period, that word 'love' will scuttle about. Ben might be sexually aroused by his wife in the morning. Over breakfast, he enjoys the silence of companionable love. At dinner, Ben jokes and laughs with his wife in friendly love before giving her a foot rub in front of the telly as a kind of committed love. 'Love' encompasses a lot.

This is exactly what Sternberg tried to formalise in his 'triangular theory' of love.

Sternberg believed that there are three basic components to love, and when you mix these up in different combinations, you can identify eight different kinds of love. The three components are:

- *Intimacy*: This is when you feel comfortable enough around someone to be yourself. You can share your most peculiar secrets and know that they'll still like you. It's about caring for one another and being there for them.

- *Passion*: This is emotional or physical arousal. But this isn't just the sexual arousal between romantic partners; it can also be the happy, giddy feeling of seeing your best friend walk into a room or the feeling of warmth when you play with your child. It's an emotional change in your being as a result of a loved one's presence.

- *Commitment*: This is a willingness to stick with the relationship, even if it goes through a rocky patch. It's when you stay put, even if your loved one is being an arse. A parent doesn't leave their child because they keep waking up at 2 a.m. A wife doesn't leave a husband because he's no longer as attractive as he once was.

Sternberg then uses these three components to identify various types of love, including toxic ones. Infatuation is when you have only passion. Empty love is when you have only commitment. Romantic love is intimacy and passion, whereas companionate love is intimacy and commitment. Consummate love is when you have all three.

Sternberg's triangular theory of love is intuitive and appealing, and it maps easily into our own lives. Choose any meaningful relationship in your life and ask how well that scores on each of the three elements. Is that a bad thing? Sometimes yes, but often not. Consummate love might be the ideal and highest form of love, but other kinds of love also have their place.

Everyday Psychology
The Cult of Celebrity

It's time for a confession: I sometimes watch videos about random people just going about their business. It began harmlessly enough – I found an interesting video of an interview that made me think and made me laugh. So, I watched a few more videos, and then I pressed 'subscribe'. Early last year, I started to watch the 'home blog' videos, by the same man. No interviews this time, just him and his girlfriend doing *things.* And so I spend hours of my own life watching other people live theirs.

It's a confession that millions and millions of people will share. YouTube, Instagram and TikTok have given rise to a new era of celebrity. We can now log in and watch our favourite personalities do absolutely anything. So, are we now obsessed with celebrities more than ever? Should I stop watching videos of a stranger ironing his shirts?

In 2011, the psychologist John Maltby gave us his 'three dimensions of celebrity worship'.

The most basic is *entertainment-social*. We're attracted to celebrities because they are entertaining. They make us laugh and keep us engrossed. The 'social' part is that we will often talk with our friends about celebrities. We can gossip about a tabloid break-up or rank our favourite actors. We tut at bad behaviour and laugh at the silly. Awareness of particular celebrities is often mutual between friends, and they make people closer.

The second stage is *intense-personal*. This is where normal celeb-watching turns into something a bit weird. It's when people start to imagine celebrities are their actual friends. Someone might say, 'We have so much in common!' or refer to a 'special bond that can't be explained in words', and they'll spend an unhealthy amount of time checking and rechecking on that celebrity.

The final stage is *borderline-pathological*. This is when someone devotes most or all of their life to obsessing over a celebrity. Their walls will be decked out with memorabilia, and they have seen, read and bought every conceivable thing that a celebrity has done. In this stage, a person might turn to stalking behaviour – constant messaging, personal requests or even in-person interactions. Maltby highlights that borderline-pathological celebrity worship might even include a willingness to break the law, for example, fighting or harming someone who dislikes their favourite celebrity.

As we say with parasocial relationships (see pages 112–13), the degree of celebrity worship will often depend on other underlying factors, such as loneliness, obsession, anxiety and so on. But this is not to say 'the cult of celebrity' is always and everywhere a bad thing. The entertainment-social stage has not only been proven to be benign but also positively beneficial to a lot of people's mental health. And so, I'm going to go and watch another home blog, happy in the knowledge that Maltby would approve.

Marcia

Find Your Tribe

Everything I know about American high schools comes filtered through film and TV. Here, high school is a kind of tribal borderland, with warring communities rivalling for supremacy. The jocks glower at the thespians. The mathletes laugh at the goths. The mean girls roll their eyes at the stoners.

High school is a time when teenagers find out who they are. They establish the values and beliefs that place them in a certain camp and give them a certain label. Even outside Hollywood's high school, our teenage years are vitally important to who we are as people. They are the formative moments that define our adult selves.

James Marcia's 'identity status' theory attempts to make sense of this hormonal maelstrom.

It's a psychological framework that focuses on adolescent development and builds upon Erik Erikson's work on psychosocial development (see pages 102-3). Marcia divides our character development - our formative years - into four types.

1. *Identity diffusion*: This is when a teenager both refuses to commit to any particular identity and isn't really looking for one anyway. It might

characterise early adolescence, but it also represents those easily blown this way and that. An identity-diffuse person will go with whatever is happening; they'll just say or do whatever is easiest with whoever they are with.

2. *Identity foreclosure*: These people won't shop around for an identity but often fall into one or find one thrust upon them. A Muslim, raised in a strictly Muslim household, will have Islamic values and behaviours thrust upon them, with no real options available. But the same is true for a child with hard-left wing parents, alternative hippy parents or strait-laced lawyer parents. The adolescent is only really presented with one path to walk. Identity foreclosure is often on the cusp of an identity crisis or some kind of breakdown – if not immediately, one day.

3. *Identity moratorium*: Moratorium adolescents are on the fence or still deciding. They're researching, watching and learning. They do quite enjoy how the artsy people talk to each other, but they also like watching football. In this stage, teenagers are actively exploring different commitments but have not yet made final choices.

4. *Identity achievement*: This status represents individuals who have gone through the identity crisis of *foreclosure*, explored the options of the *moratorium* and made commitments to specific roles or values. They have found their tribe.

Of course, no individual can be stereotyped according to the artificial delineations of a neat box. Everyone is a bit of everything. But Marcia's argument is that there comes a point – often a conscious point – when we *decide* that certain things will matter. We say no to some people and yes to others. We wear one outfit and not another. We defend one position and don't really care about others. We all have to be someone, and that's often decided in our formative years.

Feldman Barrett
Emotional Granularity

How do you know if you're feeling frustrated or grumpy? What's the difference between sadness and nostalgia? When are you anxious, but not also nervous? Emotions can be impossible to describe at times, and they're even hard to recognise when we're *feeling* them (see pages 16–17). With our writhing tangle of complex emotions, can we ever truly know what we're feeling and why we're feeling it?

This is what concerned Lisa Feldman Barrett in her 2017 book *How Emotions Are Made*. Her theory of 'emotional granularity' might be useful for all of us.

Feldman Barrett argues that we learn to differentiate our emotions by a combination of observing our environment (such as your dad swearing at your spilled milkshake) and being explicitly taught it ('Dad gets angry when you stain the carpet'). We then come to identify feelings in others, but also in ourselves.

In the theory of emotions, there are three distinct aspects:

1. *Valence*: Is it good or bad?

2. *Arousal*: How intense is it?

3. *Motivation*: Does it make me behave a certain way?

All emotions are then learned by placing them somewhere along these scales (without using that language). We might say sadness is -6 valence, 6 arousal and 3 motivation. Ecstasy is +8, 7, 4, and so on …

There are two interesting ideas packed into this.

Firstly, I might think 'anxious' is -6 valence, but you might call it -3, for instance – we don't all learn to recognise emotions in the same way.

Secondly, there is what Feldman Barrett calls 'emotional granularity', the idea that people can be better or worse at emotional literacy. Growing up, I might have learned five ways to describe 'fear' feelings; you might only have 'scared'. This is shown, too, in how children younger than three years often have difficulty separating being sad, mad or scared. They need to be taught how. They need to improve their 'emotional granularity'.

So, even having feelings isn't straightforward any more. If we want to see the world in more colour, to be aware of the detail and minutiae of our emotional universe, we have to practise. Speak to a therapist, get out a thesaurus or read some poetry. Our inner life is there to be understood, so let's learn to read it better.

Rain and Mar

Parasocial Relationships

One of the most powerful elements of a great story is how it makes us feel. People can form profound emotional connections with fictional characters. From a corseted heroine on a country estate to the wand-wafters of Hogwarts, a well-crafted character can pull us so deeply into their fictional world that we temporarily forget about the real one. But for some, those connections become especially and peculiarly strong. It is possible for people to form intimate, if somewhat one-sided, relationships with fictional characters that mirror real-life relationships. Sometimes, they might even surpass them.

We saw on pages 34–5 that the relationships we build during our formative years affect how we navigate interpersonal relationships later in life. When our early relationships are dysfunctional, such as excessive or deficient attention from our parents, we are likely to develop certain 'attachment styles'. We can explain someone's fear of commitment or clingy need for constant affirmation as being the adult manifestation of childhood learning. But there's recently been a body of research about how these attachment styles might even affect how we view fictional characters. It's the psychology of fandom.

In 2021, Marina Rain and Raymond A. Mar wrote a paper entitled 'Adult Attachment and Engagement with Fictional Characters' in which they argued that relationships formed with stories or fictional characters were surrogate parasocial activities. The study found that people with 'attachment avoidance' behaviours in real life – who consciously shun meaningful social bonds – were more likely to experience greater character identification and depend on 'parasocial *interactions*' when watching TV. In other words, if you keep real, everyday relationships at arm's length, you tend to welcome fictional characters with open arms. TV relationships play surrogate for real ones.

The situation is amplified for those with attachment anxiety – people who constantly worry their relationships aren't secure. According to the study, they were more likely to form 'parasocial *relationships*' with the characters they saw. They would tend to have a 'false sense of mutual awareness with their favourite characters and form strong emotional bonds with them'.

In other words, those with attachment avoidance tend to use fictional worlds as substitutes for a lack in their real life. People with attachment *anxiety* tend to obsess over characters and form emotional bonds. They reread comforting books and rewatch TV shows with characters they feel have the same 'mutual awareness' as them.

Opinions vary about how healthy or otherwise fandom can be. Some people will find it disturbing how aggressively online communities might defend a fictional world or find strange the amount of effort and money people give to cosplay. Others, though, will have their own kind of surrogate relationship and find it totally understandable. At the end of the day, Rain and Mar highlight a simple fact about human psychology: we all need to form relationships, even if how and where that happens might vary hugely.

Social Psychology

You're on your own in a room doing anything at all – cooking, singing, cleaning, reading, doing your laces or whatever. Suddenly, someone else walks into the room and things change. One has become two; an individual has become a group. Humans everywhere behave differently when they're together.

Social psychology is the study of what happens when people get together in groups.

Milgram
Turn It Up to Eleven

Holding a clipboard and wearing a lab coat makes you a powerful person. Add in a lanyard and a confident voice, and you can do pretty much anything. People love to obey authority. Most of the time, this is fairly harmless (even necessary for a functioning society), but it can also lead to very dark places.

Enter Stanley Milgram.

After the Second World War, people wanted to know how and why the Holocaust took place. In the USA, the public believed that the Germans were monsters for their willingness to follow such immoral orders. Milgram hoped to show how good Americans would never be so susceptible to authoritarianism.

His experiment involved three people. There was the experimenter, dressed in a lab coat, giving instructions and prompts. There was an actor, playing the role of the 'learner'. And there was the participant, who thought they were the 'teacher' in a 'memory test'. The idea was that whenever the learner got an answer wrong, the teacher would administer a shock.

As the learner made mistakes, the teacher was told to increase the voltage. A recording was played of the learner (apparently) making cries of pain and, as it went on, pleading for the shocks to stop. The teacher was told to increase the voltage to a level that was very clearly laid out as fatal – not least because the learner was desperately repeating that he had a heart condition.

The results were surprising. Sixty-five per cent of the participants were willing to give the lethal 450 volts, and they *all* administered a traumatic 300 volts. In the studies that came after, with a variety of different set-ups, that roughly two-thirds result came up again and again, showing that two out of three people would be willing to kill if told to do so by someone in authority.

But there are some problems with Milgram's experiments, and we ought to be cautious about over-hyping the results. The *majority* of teachers were deeply disturbed by what they did and physically distressed by the experiment – it wasn't as if inflicting pain came easily. And the experiment took place over a single hour, with very little time either to deliberate or talk things over with someone. In most situations, like the Holocaust, the perpetrators had ample time (years) to reflect on their actions, and yet they still chose to continue. Milgram perhaps highlights only how far we'll go in the heat of the moment.

That said, Milgram's experiment stays with us. He proved that we'll do terrible things if only someone tells us to. One silver lining to this might be in what we can learn from it. Simply knowing about Milgram helps reveal how far we can be manipulated, and that allows us to say 'no'. Knowing that authority can sometimes be wrong makes us think twice.

Everyday Psychology
The Janus-Facebook

Ron is an eighty-year-old widower. He sees his family regularly and has friends in the village, but he's lonely. He misses his wife, of course, but he also just misses people. Then, one day, Ron's son sets him up on Facebook. Now Ron messages his grandkids every day. He looks at his son's page and reads his friends' status updates. Ron doesn't talk to them, but he feels closer to them. And he doesn't feel so lonely.

Becky is fourteen years old, and she's talking to the school counsellor. She's addicted to Instagram and TikTok, and it's damaging her. Every free moment she has is spent scrolling through algorithmically determined photos and sponsored content. Becky spends five hours a day looking at slim, tanned and rich models posing on holiday. Her friends are all laughing and happy, with dreamy boyfriends and no problems. Becky has spots, hates her nose and eats only lettuce at lunch.

Social media is a Janus-faced beast. To the Rons of the world, it offers connection and distraction. To the Beckys of the world, it causes mental health conditions and stupefaction. Most of us lie somewhere in between. So, what does social media do to our psychology?

Some people really hate social media. They claim that it has ruined a generation (see page 280) or is the incontrovertible cause of the mental health crisis. But there is little evidence that there *is* a mental health crisis. Since 2003, only in America has there been an increase in suicides. In other countries we have data for, like Norway, Sweden, Denmark and the UK, the number of suicides is either the same or decreasing. In 2023, teams from Tilburg and Oxford Universities both concluded that internet connectivity (which is, admittedly, broader than just social media) might even be *bettering* people's mental health.

That said, there is also overwhelming evidence to suggest that *excessive* social media use can *increase* loneliness. It causes anxiety and depression. And, given that tech companies deliberately design their products to be as addictive as possible, the slippery slope from Ron to Becky is excessively well lubricated. Facebook wants you to come back. Instagram wants you to stay on longer. TikTok is an audio-visual sensory extravaganza that will always make the real world look dreary. Social media is built to activate all the reward systems in your brain (see page 24).

The thing about pop psychology and cod psychiatry is that it's often a reductionist polemic, fit more for a school debate. If you ever hear someone attack 'social media', get them to explain which platform and why. The vast majority of social media users are not sixteen-year-old girls with body image issues. They are friends organising a stag do, parents sharing photos of their kids, and the lonely Rons reaching out for some – any – human connection.

Asch

Copying Your Work

It's the last question of the quiz and Chloë knows the answer: it's Bolivia. Yes, definitely Bolivia. She's been there, so she ought to know. But then Shaun says it's Panama, and the others agree with him. Chloë's *sure* it's Bolivia, but Shaun's so confident and the others are nodding furiously.

'What do you think, Chloë?' she's asked.

'Yeh, Shaun's probably right. Put Panama,' she mumbles.

We've all been Chloë. Humans are social animals, spending our lives in families, tribes or workplaces. So it's no wonder that we try to fit in or conform. Animosity and rejection are not only mentally devastating, we're also biologically wired to avoid them. The lone *homo sapiens* is a dead *homo sapiens*. But this instinct can take us to ridiculous and dark places.

In the 1960s, Solomon Asch looked at this in a series of experiments.

Asch had participants do a simple task: choose which line was the longest out of three options. The right answer was obvious, one line was easily the biggest.

When alone, people chose correctly 99 per cent of the time.

Asch then put his subjects in a group with actors who were told to deliberately choose the wrong answer. In these conditions, 75 per cent of subjects agreed with the group consensus at least once, even though they were *blatantly* wrong.

A similar but more alarming 1968 study by John Darley and Bibb Latané had subjects appear for a 'job interview'. As the subjects waited, smoke was slowly pumped into the room. If they were alone, the interviewees would always check what was wrong and/or leave. Smoke was coming into the room! But when they were in a room with actors pretending that nothing was wrong, only one in ten did anything. This was despite everyone coughing and rubbing their eyes. 'Well, if these guys are all right with it, I guess it must be okay.'

What are the implications of this? Well, as Asch said, 'That intelligent, well-meaning people are willing to call white black is concerning.' Conformity has consequences beyond simply going along with a known falsehood. Will you tell a laughing group of people that a joke was sexist or racist? Or it might explain how a kind, loving man can, within a few years, be party to the genocide of six million Jews.

Conformity has no doubt made humanity great, but equally true is that it brings out the darkest and worst in us.

Festinger
Why I Hate Sam

I'm going to tell you a secret. Jeff Bezos doesn't bother me. Elon Musk doesn't bother me. All of the world's billionaires don't really bother me. Sure, on a rational level, I don't *like* them. I don't like the idea of billionaires existing in a world where there is starvation and poverty. But on a personal level? I'm not that bothered.

Sam Walton *does* bother me. I went to school with Sam, so we had a similar education and were from similar families in the same hometown. But Sam is now earning bank-swelling money with a big house and a fast car. The reason that Sam bothers me and Elon doesn't is because of what the American psychologist Leon Festinger called 'social comparison theory'.

Many of the adjectives we use to describe and understand ourselves are comparatives. I'm *rich* in comparison to a rice farmer in rural China but not in comparison to Sam. I'm *young* in comparison to my boss but not to the new intern. And my dad still thinks it hilarious to say he's average height. He was in the 1960s; he's *short* by today's standards.

So, a lot of how we understand ourselves and each other is framed by comparison. This led Festinger to argue that we *need* to compare ourselves with others if we are to have any definable traits at all.

Festinger knew that there were some objective values. My dad is 5ft 8in. I'm in my late thirties. Sam earns seven digits a year. But the problem with objective values is that most people don't care about them. They want to know where they fall on a scale. When I used to teach and I gave my pupils back their essays, the *first* thing they asked was, 'What did you get?' The absolute score, the objective number, didn't matter. They wanted to place themselves in a hierarchy. Am I better or worse than my classmates?

Height, wealth and age are all, by and large, defined by the objective measures of an external world. But what about other adjectives, like 'kind' or 'productive'? You might feel you were more productive yesterday or you did more kind things today, but these do not act as benchmarks. We need to know *how many* kind acts make you kind and *how many* emails you have to send in a morning to be called productive. And for that, we need comparisons.

It's a social media cliché to say, 'Don't care what other people think.' Live your life, and don't worry about others. But what Festinger revealed is that this is just not how we work. Most of our essential characteristics are defined by comparisons. Sam is my 'upward comparison' in some ways and my 'downward comparison' in others. You are the object of someone's jealousy and another person's pity. Comparison is the heart of identity.

Tajfel and Turner
The Importance of Cleavage

When I used to teach UK politics to sixteen-year-olds, I always looked forward to the week we learned about voting behaviours. Because I had to use the term social cleavage. Without fail, a few boys would snigger, a few girls would roll their eyes, and the rest would hide smiles. In politics, a cleavage is the way society is divided by its norms and core values. Various cleavages will correlate with certain political parties. So, in the UK, if you know someone is a church-going, high-income pensioner living in a rural area, you can pretty much bet your hat that they'll vote Conservative. Inversely, an immigrant, urban renter is overwhelmingly likely to vote Labour.

There are a million ways to divide a society. You have big divisions, like social class, religious beliefs, income levels, education, age and so on. However, there are also less well-known factors such as cultural preferences, physical fitness levels, pet ownership, and even your choice of specific platforms like Apple or Android. You can learn a lot about a person by knowing which group they belong to.

In fact, according to Henri Tajfel and John Turner, our social identity and self-esteem are almost entirely derived from the groups we sign up for.

Tajfel and Turner's social identity theory suggests that people categorise *themselves and others* into various social groups (defined by class, religion, sports teams and so on), and that we spend an inordinate amount of energy maintaining or enhancing our worth within that group. In other words, our self-esteem heavily depends on how well perceived or successful we are within the specific groups we favour. Consider Ryan, who strongly identifies as vegan. Ryan will do his utmost to be the best possible vegan he can be and will be sure to tell everyone about how great his veganism is. All other options pale in comparison to veganism. You should try it too.

Of course, not everyone will like Ryan's proselytising veganism, and social identity theory identifies this too as essential to who we are. It's known as 'comparison'. To feel like we belong and to bulwark our identity, we set ourselves up against a rival group. Vegans vs. carnivores, Arsenal vs. Chelsea, Tories vs. Labour and so on. We are defined not only by our group but also by the groups we're not.

Social identity theory reveals both our better and worse natures. On the one hand, that sense of belonging and being part of a group is what makes us supremely happy. Chanting your team's song from the stands, turning up to *your* pub on a Friday night or winning the weekly bridge game are peak experiences. On the other hand, as we see on page 127, in-group favouritism and out-group derogation are what lead to hooliganism, racism and prejudice.

Perhaps the most important 'group' to belong to is the human race?

Sherif
Rattlers and Eagles

It was 2020 in the UK, and the country was in the middle of the COVID-19 lockdown. People were isolated, scared and starting to go a little stir-crazy. The media was full of heartwarming stories – clapping for nurses, food donations and neighbourhood spirit. But then, someone with a camera and Twitter noticed something odd: the supermarkets were running out of toilet paper. Shelves normally full of Andrexian white puppies were now dusty and barren. The country went into hysterics. A meltdown in the lockdown. People were buying up fifty rolls at a time, pushing trolleys full of toilet paper towers to their small hatchback cars. Rationing was brought in. Paranoia and suspicion took hold.

'That's quite a big shopping bag you've got there, Val. Wouldn't be hoarding bog roll, would you?'

The 2020 toilet roll panic buy was just one tiny punctuation mark in a very long book of conflict. It was all about competition over scarce resources, and according to Muzafer Sherif, it's one of the most important reasons for conflict there is.

In 1954, Sherif did an experiment that put *Lord of the Flies* to shame. He took a bunch of twelve-year-old boys out into Robbers Cave State Park in Oklahoma and put them into two groups. They were given tasks, rewards and objectives. Today, it would probably be on Channel 5 and hosted by some C-list celebrities. What happened was that the groups quickly formed an identity. They formed a culture and social norms. They gave themselves names: the Rattlers and the Eagles. They even made and planted a flag with a sign saying: 'KEEP OUT!'

After about five days of this, the two groups were brought together to compete for food and prizes. It was pandemonium. A vicious, testosterone-fuelled rumble royale ensued. When the name-calling, denigration and mockery gave way to fists, the researchers were forced to step in. Adults with clipboards had to hold back flailing Eagles and swinging Rattlers.

Sherif rightly concluded from this that most conflict is born of two, often related, phenomena: 'in-group' vs. 'out-group' mentality catalysed by resource scarcity. The Rattlers and Eagles might have got along okay, were it not for the fight for limited goods.

But arguably more important than this was how the experiment concluded. The groups were reconciled. Conflict was abated and friendships were restored. How? By getting the groups to come together for mutual benefit. Get them to cooperate on tasks and the 'us' vs. 'them' is dissolved. So, the next time you have a fight with someone or you have two children squabbling over trinkets, try to do something together. Fight a mutual foe and you'll be best of friends before you can say 'unethical child experiments'.

Everyday Psychology
Marking Your Tribe

In the transitional warmth of late summer, two German tourists were out for a walk in the Ötztal Alps. It was your classic alpine walk. A stunning panorama, a gentle breeze ... and the discovery of the upper torso of a 5,000-year-old corpse. The archaeological world went bananas for 'Ötzi', and the media weren't too far behind. Here was a glacially preserved body from the Neolithic period, a window into our ancestral past. One among many curious discoveries was that Ötzi had at least sixty tattoos.

Ötzi is proof that we've been marking our skin and modifying our bodies since we lost our hair and came down from the trees. But why are humans so taken with tattoos?

Everyone who gets a tattoo will have a different reason. If you ask why, you'll get a story, and often a heartfelt and moving story, too. I remember once spending the better part of an evening as a friend of mine – tattooed almost from neck to feet – told me the individual tale behind each and every one. It was an autobiographical journey across his body, and it was enchanting. So, on one level at least, tattoos serve as a tapestry or signpost for a life.

Historically, tattoos often served to mark you out as a certain kind of person. Tattoos would be given to the initiated, they marked the 'ins' from the 'outs'. Prisoners in Russian gulags used to tattoo their crimes as a defiant inversion of the shame of branding. Soldiers would tattoo their regiment or unit. A tribe would mark themselves with sacred runes. In 2022, a team from the University of Tennessee developed the psychology of tattooing in line with social identity theory (see page 125). They discovered that a tattoo's 'uniqueness positively influenced group identity but not self-identity'. Paradoxically, getting their own tattoo – a unique and particular act – marked people as part of a group, not set apart as an independent person. The same paper went on to show how those who had tattoos felt a greater sense of spirituality. Tattooing is a kind of ritual initiation.

Of course, there's still a certain stigma attached to tattoos today. If you commit yourself to one group or identity, that will, by definition, alienate other groups of people. But more than that, tattoos have often been associated with rebellion against society. Historically, psychiatric patients, drug addicts and criminals were far more likely to have tattoos than the general population. But of course that doesn't mean the tattooed these days are more likely to be mentally ill.

Tattoos, like fashion, play an important role in constructing who we are. Those who get tattoos will often do so as a statement of belonging – this is who I am, and this is what matters. It's a visual and public display of your identity.

Darley and Latané
Watching Someone Die

In May 2023, an ex-US marine named Daniel Penny killed a black homeless man named Jordan Neely. Dozens of people watched Penny do it. Neely was mentally ill, shouting threatening things and making people generally uneasy. Penny approached him from behind and put Neely in a chokehold. After several minutes, Neely died. He died with dozens of people watching, and no one stepped in to help. No one even told Penny to stop. Later, some witnesses claimed regret. Others admitted to being scared to step in.

The killing of Jordan Neely is one of the more recent examples of an ancient phenomenon: the bystander effect.

This theory, identified by John Darley and Bibb Latané in 1968, suggests that individuals are less likely to help a victim when other people are present. More than anything, the bystander effect is all about the *diffusion of responsibility*. When you stand in a crowd, you lose yourself. You feel you are all collectively responsible and all collectively free of responsibility.

Perhaps more important than the fact of a bystander effect is how to avoid it. For this, Darley and Latané identified a five-step model of bystander intervention, which is to say, these are the five things that need to be true if someone is to step in.

First, you must notice the event. You can't intervene if you can't see what's going on.

Second, you must recognise the event as an emergency. With Jordan Neely, it's perfectly possible that people thought Penny was restraining but not killing Neely. Likewise, a domestic argument between a wife and husband might be *seen as* harmless, though it might actually escalate quickly. There is a strange phenomenon known as 'pluralistic ignorance', which is where we often don't call something an emergency, even when it clearly is, because other people seem okay with it.

Third, you must assume some responsibility. This is what is most lacking in the group context. When others are present and equally qualified, why should you, specifically, be the one responsible for fixing the situation?

Fourth, you must feel able to help. The bystander effect is not about a crowd of people unable to rush a terrorist gunman who is brandishing a rifle them.

Fifth, a person must decide to act. Sometimes, they might not act due to fear, for example, of the risk of being harmed if they step in to stop a fight. Sometimes, it might be because of self-consciousness, when being the one to get involved puts them centre stage and at risk of being judged.

It's easy to be judgemental in cases of the bystander effect: how could decent people *not* stop something horrendous from happening? But it requires huge moral courage to step forward and to shoulder responsibility. The individual who does intervene has to fight the collective weight of everyone else who didn't. That's incredibly hard. It's heroic.

Zimbardo

Why Psychology is Hard

The Stanford Prison Experiment (SPE) rivals Pavlov's dogs (see pages 174–5) for being *the* most famous study in psychology history. It's paradoxically so shocking and yet so understandable. The experiment proved that if you give most humans the right opportunity, they will do great evil. The devils on our shoulders are only waiting for the power and excuse to take charge. The SPE leaves us with a guilty revelation: most of us would have been Nazis if we'd lived in 1930s Germany.

But Philip Zimbardo's SPE might not be as straightforward as we think.

The 1971 experiment sought to investigate the psychological effects of power in the wake of the Second World War. It was a simulation where volunteers were randomly assigned to the role of either 'guard' or 'prisoner' within a mock prison environment. The study was meant to last for two weeks but things didn't go according to plan. On the second day, the first participant had to be released because of 'acute emotional disturbance'. The entire thing had to be cancelled after six days. The guards adopted cruel and authoritarian measures and subjected the prisoners to very real psychological torture, while the prisoners exhibited extreme stress, passivity and emotional trauma.

But all is not as it seems. In 2019, the French psychologist Thibault Le Texier released a paper entitled 'Debunking the Stanford Prison Experiment'. In it, Le Texier lists reasons to challenge the results of the experiment, for example: 'Zimbardo designed his experiment from the outset as a demonstration of the toxicity' and 'the guards were given clear instructions for how to create this pathogenic social environment'. For Le Texier, the experiment would fail most modern checks, and its results should be seen as highly suspect.

The question then becomes: if the SPE is so famous and important but flawed, why has no one tried to repeat it? This raises two lingering issues in psychology generally.

The first is about ethics. So many experiments before the 1980s were unequivocally immoral. They had inadequate safeguards, traumatised victims, and involved dubious or no consent whatsoever. While new ethical standards are obviously for the good, they do limit the range and depth of a lot of psychology, especially social psychology.

The second concerns psychology's 'replicability crisis'. It's really hard to reproduce results because each time you repeat an experiment, you're dealing with different experimenters and different participants at a different time. And if we can't replicate experimental results, it's hard to take a scientific conclusion seriously.

So, while Zimbardo's experiment is popular, it is often misleadingly presented. Perhaps the biggest result of the SPE is to show how limited scientifically rigorous social psychology can be.

Jung
Archetypes

The *Commedia dell'Arte* is one of the earliest examples of professional theatre in the world. It was popular around the sixteenth century in Italy, and it was famous for a recognisable cast of stereotypes. For all the various and magical tales the actors would tell, the cast was almost always made up of *types*. There would be Zanni, the clown, and Vecchi, the rich, miserly lord. Today, most of the TV shows and movies we watch have something similar. The brooding, tortured lead and their bouncy comic-relief sidekick. The high-functioning savant (see page 90) and the gormless dead wood they run rings around.

But what if life were not so different? What if life had these typecast characters too?

For the pioneering Swiss psychiatrist Carl Jung, archetypes are 'archaic or primordial types with universal images that have existed since the remotest times'. They pop up again and again in myth, fables, folk psychology and our collective unconscious. Archetypes are not people as such, but they describe the different modes in which people behave. They are like masks or costumes in a play.

Nowadays, a whole folklorist's trove of archetypes have been identified – we have tricksters, rebels, wizards, lovers and so on. But Jung never formally provided a definitive list. Broadly, and through squinted eyes, we can identify the following OG Jungian archetypes:

- *The Mother*: A caring, life-affirming and nurturing creator.
- *The Child or Maiden*: An innocent, pure, hopeful naïf.
- *The Wise Old Man*: The sage, intelligent, sensible voice of reason.
- *The Shadow*: The destructive and fractious rebel who breaks the world for a laugh.
- *The Animal*: A personification of the lustful, passionate, biological impulses we have inside us.

While the terms are gendered, the archetypes are not. A father can be a Mother, and a boy can be a Maiden. What's more, a world-tempered youth can be a Wise Old Man, and a great many adults are still a Child. The archetypes are fluid: real-life humans don't fall into the neat categories of a Buzzfeed quiz. Everyone embodies elements of each, and they may vary across their lifetime.

Jungian archetypes sit awkwardly in academia. They have no empirical data to support them, so they are not science. They are more proclamation than argument, so they are not philosophy. What they are, though, is *hugely* popular. And this popularity alone, not to mention their repeated appearance in the stories we've told each other since ancient times, might lead us to take them seriously.

Mischel

More than a Social Media Bio

Weddings are often stressful, highly fraught events. The planning is bad enough. Everything is expensive, and every decision seems simultaneously too important and far too trivial. Then there's the politics of it all. You can't have Uncle Winny sit anywhere near Auntie Brenda ever since *that* Christmas. But one of the more unforeseen worries of a wedding is known as 'context collapse'.

Context collapse is what happens when all your various personalities are forced to perform at the same time. Let's say that Ed is getting married. To his wedding, he invites his schoolmates, who know him as a drunken clown. He invites his colleagues, who know him as a strait-laced accounts guy. He invites his family, who know him as the cute boy who always liked to climb on things. He invites his wife's friends, who know him as polite but standoffish. Suddenly, under one roof, he has to be all things to everyone.

Moments of context collapse highlight an important part of our personalities. It's something the Austrian-born psychologist Walter Mischel talked a lot about.

Mischel challenged the traditional view of personality as a set of fixed traits, arguing instead that behaviour is highly dependent on situational contexts. It makes no sense to talk about someone as being shy, for example; better to say that they are shy in certain contexts and with certain people. Everyone exhibits different behaviours in different situations.

The reason this is important is because there is a multi-billion-pound industry in 'personality assessment'. Corporations and educational bodies want to know what kind of person you are. Mischel's point is that these will always create artificial boxes to jam you in. Imagine you take a personality test. A question like 'Do you tend to prefer large or smaller groups?' forces you to come down on either side. I prefer large groups, in the main. But the question is a false dichotomy and an oversimplification. I prefer a large group of my family to a small group of people I hate. I prefer a large group at a wedding and a small group playing board games. Personality is all about context, framing and particulars rather than 'traits'.

Mischel's work has two interesting implications. The first is obvious. No one can be easily reduced to a string of personality traits, and your complex inner life isn't a slave to personality dispositions. The second, though, is more tricky. If there is no such thing as personality, does it make sense to talk about 'traits' at all? The words 'shy', 'confident', 'timid', 'buffoonish', 'polite' and so on do mean something, but what do they mean in Mischel's framework? The answer has to do with tendencies. How *often* are you shy? If presented with situation X, do you tend to be polite or straight-talking?

Do you think you possess certain traits? Or does saying so reduce you a bit?

Goffman
The World's a Stage

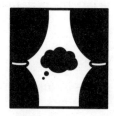

Erving is on holiday in the Shetland Islands. He's booked into the same hotel he always stays at and is enjoying a well-poached egg. Erving is alone, and he's watching the hotel staff. He's amused by how differently the staff behave when they're talking to the guests and when they're behind the bar or in the kitchen – when they *think* they're not being seen. In the restaurant, the staff are demure, servile, respectful. 'Yessir, straight away, sir. I shall speak to Chef.' The moment they think they are unseen, it's first names, banter and normal conversations.

This true story is what inspired the twentieth-century social psychologist Erving Goffman to coin the terms 'backstage' and 'front stage' behaviours.

It's hardly fresh material to say 'all the world's a stage'. Shakespeare might have popularised the phrase but the idea is as old as the written word. Today, it's repeated often enough to proudly sit among other clichés – but, as with most clichés, it contains more than a codpiece of truth. As Goffman put it, 'All the world is not, of course, a stage, but the crucial ways in which it isn't are not easy to specify.'

Goffman's 'dramaturgical perspective' sees life as a never-ending play with individuals acting on the societal stage. Each of us will play multiple roles in our daily lives, like a theatre actor playing different characters. These roles can range from social identities, as in 'friend' or 'spouse', to professional ones, such as 'intern' or 'manager'. The performance of these roles depends on who the audience is and the social context. I am a dad. I talk openly about poo, wee and disgusting bodily functions with my young son. That's my role. When I go into the office, it would be a strange thing to ask my boss if he needs help on the toilet. It's a different stage with different actors.

All of which isn't especially new wisdom. Where Goffman differentiates his theory, though, is in the idea of 'backstage' and 'front stage' behaviours. In the 1940s, the philosopher Jean-Paul Sartre talked about 'the gaze' of others – where we radically alter not only our behaviours but also our sense of self when others are watching. Goffman, though, does not think there is an 'authentic' self to return to. There is no raw *you*. Rather, our backstage behaviours are themselves either a performance or the preparation for a performance.

Goffman's dramaturgical perspective is both a cliché and a cliché buster. Yes, it's eye-rollingly trite to say, 'I feel like an actor.' What's interesting, though, is to add, 'But that's what life is – acting is a part of being human.' It's not duplicitous to talk politely to guests but make lewd jokes to your colleagues. It's not fake to talk about the weather with Granny but football with your friends. It's being human.

Cialdini
Selling Ice to Eskimos

In the fourth century BCE, Aristotle wrote his book *Rhetoric*, an ancient Greek guide to getting your own way. It was about oration, persuasion and manipulation. Aristotle was a virtuous man, so he sneered at sophistry and baulked at using his tricks for evil. Fast forward 2,500 years, and people are still at it, but with decidedly less virtue.

Aristotle, Cicero and Machiavelli wrote a lot about how to influence people, but in the twentieth century, persuasion put on a lab coat and got some data to back things up. And the biggest name in persuasion psychology is Robert Cialdini.

In the 1980s, Cialdini spent three years working in three of the most persuasive industries in the world: used car dealerships, telemarketing firms and fundraising organisations. He watched, learned and recorded what made someone good or bad at their job, how they managed to pin down a sale or a donation.

In his book *Influence: The Psychology of Persuasion*, Cialdini identified six key elements of persuasion.

- *Reciprocity*: There's a reason free samples work. Not only do they show off the wares but they also establish a subtle debt dynamic. 'This person has given me a free olive, so I should probably buy five jars of them.'

- *Consistency*: People don't like to contradict themselves. If they've committed in the past, they feel they have to commit in the future. 'Hello, I noticed that you said you'd be willing to give to cancer charities on our Facebook survey. Well, here I am!'

- *Authority*: 'Nine out of ten dentists choose our toothpaste!' If a product or service has gravitas to it, you're more likely to buy it. It need not be experts; it could also be a celebrity.

- *Scarcity*: If people think something is 'limited edition' or soon to run out, they really want it. This can often lead to conflict and bitterness (see page 127), but it also makes for great sales psychology.

- *Social proof*: Have you noticed that if you walk into an empty restaurant, they will often put you by the window? It's not because it's the best seat. It's because the manager wants other people to see you. If other people are wondering where to eat, the social proof that other people think this restaurant is good might draw them in.

- *Liking*: If you build a rapport with someone and they genuinely like you, you're more likely to get a sale. It's why that man is cracking jokes and acting like he's your brother; it might even be why the waitress is gently flirting with you.

There you have the tricks. Now it's up to you to use them to change the world for the better or exploit it as much as you can.

Kahneman

Why People Stay in Toxic Relationships

Your boss calls you into her office to tell you that you're getting a £3,000 pay rise. On a scale of one to ten, how happy would you be?

Now imagine your boss calls you to in say you're getting a £3,000 pay cut. On a scale of one to ten, how upset would you be?

For most people, the unhappiness from the pay cut would be greater than the happiness from the raise. This asymmetry is a central insight of Daniel Kahneman and Amos Tversky's 'prospect theory'. This is the idea that we are loss-averse by default and feel the sting of a loss *twice* as strongly as the pleasure of an equivalent gain.

Prospect theory can help explain our decision-making under uncertainty. Let's look at one depressingly common example: why do many people stay in unhappy relationships? First, the pain of perceived losses (emotional or financial difficulties, changes in social status and so on) *seems* to outweigh the potential gains of ending the relationship (peace of mind, independence).

Second, what Kahneman and Tversky revealed is that we're risk-seeking when it comes to how desperately we want to avoid a loss. So, most people will prefer to hold out for an uncertain win than receive a certain loss. The unhappy spouse might convince themselves that their *current* lack of happiness could one day reverse itself, so they hang on rather than face the certain loss of the relationship. 'Oh, it's a phase,' they'll say, or, 'It'll be better when X, Y, or Z happens.' The rainbow is just over the horizon.

The flipside of this is that we're risk-averse when it comes to protecting gains. We convince ourselves that the guarantee of having a partner, no matter how bad, is better than the *potential* gains of ending the relationship.

The good news, though, is that prospect theory also gives us great power to reframe our choices so we can make better decisions.

For instance, the £3,000 pay cut made us angry because we saw it as £3,000 less than the reference point of our existing salary. But if we change our reference point to zero ('I'm lucky I have a job at all in this economy'), then the cut loses its sting.

Similarly, changing our focus from our current self (who wants to do the easy thing) to our future self (who'll thank us for having done the hard thing) can help us leave bad relationships and make better decisions in general.

Haidt
Moral Dilemmas

Chris is having drinks with an old school friend, a friend who's always been at Chris's side and has helped him through some dark years. At the third drink, his friend leans over and confesses he's been robbing houses. He's been at it for a few months now. Should Chris tell the police?

Kate is at her husband's bedside. He's dying. He's wired to various screens and full of needles and tubes. The metronomic beep-beep-beep of the machines is broken only by her husband's wheezing breath. Last month, when Kate's husband was conscious, he told her he didn't want to live like this. 'Turn off the machine,' he said. But she doesn't want to hurt him. The doctors are doing their best. What should Kate do?

We all have our own moral dilemmas to deal with. They are those painful moments in life where two paths – both with their own persuasions – diverge. We are forced to walk only one way, and neither way looks perfect. For the writer and psychologist Jonathan Haidt, moral dilemmas of this kind usually arise because of a conflict between five innate 'moral foundations'. These foundations are essential to who we are.

Haidt believed that there are certain evolutionary and natural reasons underpinning our moral beliefs. We are social animals who need to live in groups to survive. And so, we have five innate, modular moral foundations that influence our intuitive ethical responses:

1. *Care/harm:* This is related to our evolution as mammals with attachment systems (see pages 34–5) and the ability to feel and dislike the pain of others. It underlies virtues like kindness and nurturing.

2. *Fairness/cheating*: Evolving from reciprocal altruism, this foundation is about justice and rights.

3. *Loyalty/betrayal*: Stemming from the need to live in tribes, this foundation is about patriotism and self-sacrifice for the group.

4. *Authority/subversion*: Society needs hierarchical social interactions, and so this foundation is about leadership, respect for authority and tradition.

5. *Sanctity/degradation*: Influenced by the psychology of disgust and contamination, this foundation is about living an elevated, noble life and includes virtues like self-discipline and spirituality.

Our opening stories involve conflicts in these foundations. Chris is torn between loyalty and fairness or authority. Kate is torn between harm and loyalty to her husband and the sanctity of his right to death.

Haidt is keen to point out that while these are all natural to humans generally, the emphasis and manifestation of these foundations will often depend on our cultural heritage. For instance, when Haidt travelled to India, he was struck by how much more attuned to sanctity or purity the Indian people were compared to his own, Western, context.

So, which of the five are you most sensitive to?

Triplett

Abracadabra!

A man stands in front of a class of young students. He's wearing top hat and tails, white gloves and a slick, oily moustache. He's a clichéd stage magician in the days before it was a cliché. The man throws a ball in the air. He throws it again. Then he throws it again. The kids look at each other in confusion. This isn't that impressive. Then, on the fifth throw, the ball vanishes. It disappears into the ether and the children gasp. The room is hushed. The magician smiles.

The year is 1900, and in the corner of the room stands the American psychologist Norman Triplett, studying what's going on.

To be a good magician, you have to understand a lot about human psychology. You have to know how perception, attention and memory work. You need to be highly attuned to our various biases and tendencies. And then you manipulate them all. You misdirect and deceive, directing people's focus this way and that. The reason that most of us enjoy a magician's stage act is because it feels as if they've got into our heads and mischievously thrown a few things about.

According to Triplett, almost all conjuring tricks depend on two maxims: expectancy and repetition. And the latter often affects the former. A magician is well-equipped to manipulate our expectations. For example, you have been conditioned over many years to watch a raised hand or to look where a pointed finger points. You've learned, too, to focus on the loud, garish and exciting. So, when the magician points or flaunts some prop, it's easy for their other hand to palm a coin or whisk away some cards unnoticed.

Sometimes, though, a magician needs to establish expectancy, and for that they use repetition. As Triplett put it, 'First actually do what the spectators are to be led to believe you do ... make a genuine experiment several times, then, when the association has been formed by repetition, a pretended experiment is made and the subject, by reason of the suggestion, responds as before.' In our opening example, the magician established association by repeatedly throwing the ball. The kids then expected to see the ball fly up again. When it didn't – the magician had whisked it away into his pocket – they *thought* they saw it disappear. The magician was using our brain's heuristics against us.

If psychology is about trying to predict and understand human behaviour, then magicians are the best psychologists there are. They can step inside the minds of an entire auditorium full of people. They can control our focus and make us believe the impossible. Magicians were playing on our cognitive biases for millennia before the likes of Daniel Kahneman and Amos Tversky came along (see page 55). It's a reminder that some of the best psychology you can find is not in the laboratory but in the everyday world.

Kübler-Ross
You're Using It Wrong

The 'five stages of grief' is probably one of the most common examples of psychology gone mainstream you'll find in this book. It's often used to refer to someone who has been bereaved, but rarely to their face. 'Oh, that's Greg; his wife died last year, and he's only just got rid of all her stuff. I think he's finally in the acceptance stage.' At other times, it gets used jokingly. 'I can't believe Chelsea lost. I think I'm in the denial phase, mate.'

The problem, though, is that for such a common idea, it's almost always used incorrectly.

In 1969, the psychiatrist Elisabeth Kübler-Ross wrote *On Death and Dying*, in which she laid out the process by which people deal with grief and tragedy. Her five stages were developed after interviewing over 200 patients recently diagnosed with a terminal illness. The initial problem, then, is that Kübler-Ross never intended her stages to be about bereavement – they were about receiving life-changing, traumatic news. The 'grief' was of those still alive, not those mourning their lost loved ones. (Which is why the 'bargaining' stage never seemed to fit.)

Furthermore, Kübler-Ross never intended this to be a rigorous science. This was not an empirical data collection exercise; this was simply a theory based on conversations she had had, however deeply psychoanalytic they might have been.

But, whether they've been misappropriated or not, Kübler-Ross's stages clearly resonate with people. Millions of people over the years have mapped their grief onto these stages. So, what are they?

1. *Denial*: In shock and disbelief, people often try to minimise the overwhelming pain of loss. They may be unable to process the reality of the situation or feel numb.

2. *Anger*: People may feel that their loss is unfair and wonder why *they* are experiencing such pain. The resultant anger is often directed towards others.

3. *Bargaining*: Individuals try to change the circumstances or make deals to prevent the loss or to alleviate the pain associated with it.

4. *Depression*: The reality of the loss sets in, bringing anguish. The griever may feel overwhelmed by the weight of their emotions and struggle to find meaning in their situation.

5. *Acceptance*: Often the 'final stage', in which individuals come to terms with their loss. This does not mean that they are no longer grieving per se, but rather that they have accepted the situation. They begin to find meaning in their loss and start to rebuild their lives.

Grief is complex, and clearly not everyone will neatly map their grief onto these five stages. In fact, trying to mould our feelings to fit them might even be harmful. But, for many, they are a helpful diagnostic tool and scaffold. They're a way to at least try and understand a period of life which often feels disorienting.

Biological Psychology

If you ask a psychologist to explain any human behaviour, they can do so in three ways. First, they can explain the social and environmental factors that lead to doing that thing. Second, they can talk about what might be going on inside a person's head – the feelings, thoughts and moods that motivate them. Finally, they can talk about neurons firing, hormones releasing and synapses working together.

It's that last one we're focusing on here: biological psychology is concerned with the physiology of the brain.

Damasio
The Heart-led Brain

According to Buzzfeed, I'm an emotional kind of guy. Using their peer-reviewed, data-led research, I answered a series of questions about Disney characters and favourite holiday locations, only to find out that I'm all emotion. Ever since, my days have been a frenzy of passion. I laugh at inappropriate things, I swear at the TV, and I can't be bothered to look after my toddler. There's no room for calculated thought any more. I've lost all my filters or social niceties; impulse is my middle name.

But, after reading Antonio Damasio's idea of 'somatic markers', I've had cause to doubt Buzzfeed's reputability.

In the Western intellectual tradition, we have inherited an idea, owed mostly to the Greeks, that emotion and reason are mirror opposites. We have feelings and thoughts; we are Dionysius vs. Apollo. Yet the Portuguese neuroscientist Antonio Damasio offers a counterpoint. Somatic markers are physiological responses that guide our decision-making. In other words, they are emotions that determine our reasoning.

For example, let's imagine Olga has only ever been in toxic relationships; every partner she's had has been abusive. As such, she's developed certain somatic markers whenever she experiences toxic behaviours in her partners. When someone puts her down, is dismissive or is peculiarly secretive about certain things, Olga has a visceral, bodily response. Her heart races, her head aches, her palms sweat, she doesn't sleep and so on.

Damasio's point is that these markers will go on to influence how we make a decision. Olga might call her partner out on their behaviour, or she might simply run for the hills. We find somatic markers in any walk of life – any major decision-making that involves 'history'. Our past encounters with X or Y will determine how we *bodily and emotionally* respond to re-encountering X or Y in the future. Our feelings set the parameters of our deliberation.

Anecdotally, this makes sense. Have you ever been in a situation where you 'can't think straight'? Or a time when being around someone or in a certain place makes you think a certain way? That's a somatic marker in action.

There is no emotion vs. reason. There is emotion-steeped reason and reason-controlled emotion. I'm off to send an angry email to Buzzfeed.

Sperry
Right and Left Brain

It's a fact known by clairvoyants and snake-oil dealers since the dawn of time: people love to categorise themselves. From Tarot cards to Myers-Briggs, we all love to say, 'Oh, I'm this kind of person.' Aquarians are highly intellectual; Type As are very determined; visual learners can't possibly sit through a lecture. With very few exceptions, these are almost all reductionist quackery. Which is a good thing, isn't it? Wouldn't it be depressing if the complexity of your human consciousness could be reduced to Mars aligning with Saturn? Would you want to be the same personality type as half the human race?

One of the more stubborn of these delineations is 'right vs. left brain' people. It all goes back to the 1960s, to the work of Roger W. Sperry, who was, to be fair, trying to actually do science.

Sperry was a neuroscientist working with patients with severe epilepsy. A popular treatment at the time was to perform a 'split brain' operation, where the corpus callosum connecting the two hemispheres is severed. But Sperry noticed something odd. Yes, the epilepsy was often cured or ameliorated, but his patients also developed altered language and spatial awareness capacities. This led him to hypothesise that each hemisphere is responsible for different cognitive functions.

Sperry set out to prove his idea by presenting stimuli to one hemisphere at a time. His research uncovered that the left hemisphere plays a pivotal role in language processing, analytical thought and logic. In contrast, the right hemisphere excels in spatial reasoning, facial recognition and the interpretation of non-verbal cues. This dichotomy was starkly illustrated in patients with split brains, where each hemisphere seemed to operate as 'a conscious system in its own right, perceiving, thinking, remembering, reasoning, willing and emoting'.

And so, a cottage industry of pseudoscience emerged. The left brain somehow became equated with logic and reasoning, the right brain with creativity and imagination. Spock was a left-brain kind of person. David Bowie had an oversized right hemisphere.

The biggest problem with Sperry's work is that it's proven to be mostly bunk. It's true that some areas of the brain are more likely to be used for certain tasks. But modern science hammers two nails into the Sperry coffin. First, almost all of the brain is used almost all the time for almost all tasks. Your left hemisphere doesn't grab a cuppa while you're singing a song. Second, if you damage a part of your brain, the other areas will, over time, adapt. In a lot of cases, you can relearn certain cognitive tasks.

That said, psychology is hugely indebted to Sperry for opening up this cranial can of worms. He called attention to the fact that parts of the brain are often better at different things. He revolutionised brain mapping and neuroscience. Which is a very left-brained thing to do.

Everyday Psychology
The Best Slice of Pizza

Five years ago, I paid a lot of money to eat in the dark. There's a restaurant chain called Dans Le Noir where you sit in a pitch-black room and eat very nice food. The idea behind it is that if you cut out visual distractions, you can focus more fully on the dinner in front of you. The food was good, and the memory of it has stuck, but I won't return to Dans Le Noir. I'm not saying they're wrong, I just think it would have been better with cutlery.

What Dans Le Noir got right, though, is that our minds play a huge role in how we enjoy and relate to our food.

You may not have heard of the gustatory system, but it's what adds a bit of spice to your world. Let's say you place some food in your mouth. Your olfactory (smell), somatosensory (touch) and gustatory (taste) receptors work together to translate the chemicals in the food into distinct signals. These signals are relayed to the brain, which separates, evaluates and distinguishes them, leading to the experience known as 'flavour'.

That's a normal, healthy, perfectly functioning gustatory story. But there's a platterful of ways it can go wrong.

First, if you're in a bad mood, then your sense of taste will be off. A 2015 study from Cornell University found a strange thing: 'During times of negative affect in our study, foods of a less pleasurable nature become even more unappealing to taste, whereas more hedonically pleasing foods remain pleasurable.' Which is to say that when we're stressed, anxious or feeling down, salads or healthy foods will taste worse. But chips, chocolate and ice cream are just as yummy. And so we reach for the Ben & Jerry's. A 2018 study by Lv et al. showed something similar happens with sleep deprivation.

Second, if you've already eaten a lot of food in the run-up to eating, your brain will dial down the intensity of the flavours. The fourth slice of pizza actually tastes worse than the first. Interestingly, there's evidence to suggest that this 'satiety' occurs in different parts of the brain for men and women, which means some foods will make women feel fuller than men.

Finally, there is the fact that some people really are wired differently when it comes to both taste intensities and satiety. This makes sense given the existence of 'supertasters' – the wine tasters and food critics of the world. But it also raises the question of whether obesity is a choice or not. Food consumption is elective, but some people feel full quicker, and some people crave sugar. That's a biological, gustatory fact. Yes, willpower might have the final say, but the *amount* of willpower required will vary hugely.

Lashley

The Search for the Holy Grail

Sometimes you discover more on the journey than you do at the destination. The real treasure was the friendships you made along the way. And this is true in science as in life. In the history of science, we can find many examples of researchers stumbling over something remarkable when they were actually looking for something else entirely. Percy Spencer was trying to improve radar and he developed the microwave. Wilhelm Conrad Röntgen was working on improved lightbulbs and gave us the X-ray.

So, too, with Karl Lashley, whose misguided, fruitless search ended up redefining neuroscience.

In the 1940s and early 1950s, Lashley was looking for the 'engram' – a specific part of the brain that was believed to hold specific memories. Very early psychology was partially influenced by the pseudoscience of phrenology. People believed that certain parts of the brain were responsible for particular cognitive processes (and character traits). The engram was the supposed centre of memory. And in his heroic search for this neuroscientific holy grail, Lashley lobotomised rats.

Lashley had rats complete a maze – something which happens peculiarly often in this book. He turned the rats into maze masters. He made absolutely sure the rats could remember the best path out of the maze. Then he performed tiny brain surgeries on the rats to remove various parts of the brain. He hoped that he would be able to identify the engram by the behaviour of the rats who were missing it.

But other than the ones who were seriously damaged by the surgery, the rats stubbornly continued to master the maze. Some took a few moments to reorientate themselves and others were a bit groggy, but Lashley just couldn't identify a single part of the brain responsible for memory.

Through this nil-result, this failed adventure, Lashley made two major contributions to psychology. The first is the idea of 'mass action', or distributed memory. Our learning does not exist in a single area but is distributed widely across the brain and various cognitive centres. The second is 'equipotentiality', which is our brain's capacity to adapt and compensate for damage to another part. For example, it's plausible that Lashley did once lobotomise the maze-memory of a rat, but the rat's brain stepped up. It took the distributed memory and rebuilt it in a new area. It learned to do it another way.

Lashley's was another deathblow to the ham-fisted, simplistic view of the brain that phrenology sold. He showed that the brain is complex and adaptable, and that neuroscience is a tricky game. There is still a lot we don't know about memories. We don't entirely know how they're stored or where, and how a biochemical, synaptic connection becomes a mental image is a question for philosophy. The good news, though, is that your brain has backed up the important stuff all around your head.

Hebb

Desire Paths in the Brain

I'm fascinated by desire paths, those man- or animal-made paths that emerge from constant rewalking. They might be a shortcut across some grass to the supermarket, or they might be a meandering trail in the woods. They are the echoey footsteps of lives that have gone before. When you walk a desire path, you are walking the collective memory of hundreds of other beings.

It turns out our actual memories are no different. Our brains are criss-crossed with a million desire paths. These are the synaptic connections we've established through repetition and constant use. And the idea goes back to Canadian psychologist Donald O. Hebb.

In 1949, Hebb gave us his famous principle that 'neurons that fire together, wire together'. Hebb's research into the brain suggested that experiences reinforce connections between neurons. When we use the brain in a particular way, we will fire off certain cells. When cells are fired in the same sequence and in the same areas, then they will form connections with each other. These connections will be few and weak at first, but as more and more synapses are formed, the brain gets much more efficient at doing what you want. This means that if neuron A consistently helps fire neuron B the synapse from A to B will become more efficient at transmitting signals.

When you first learn to play the guitar, you feel like a fumbling, awkward robot. Everything requires effort, and you're pretty sure your ring finger doesn't have that kind of dexterity. Give it three months of hard practice, though, and you'll be belting out sea shanties in time for the Folk Week open mic night.

Hebb's account of neural connections makes sense evolutionarily. Say what you like about humans but we are a hugely adaptive species. We live in mountains and tundra and deserts and swamps. If our brains didn't adapt to the constant reinforcement of our environment (see pages 174–5 on conditioning), then we'd be dead before you could say 'rigidity'.

Let's return to our desire path analogy. There used to be a tradition in the British countryside where an axe or blade would be kept at one end of a public path. It was seen as everyone's responsibility to take the blade and hack at the surrounding vegetation to keep the path clear. The way needed pruning. What Hebb revealed is that the same is true for our brains. If you want to be good at something – if you want the path to be clear – you have to keep at it. Take your mental axe and hack a neural path.

Kandel
Stroking Sea Slugs

In 1984, the philosopher Derek Parfit presented the 'teletransporter' thought experiment. Imagine a powerful device that scans every part of your body – every atom that makes up who you are, from the top of your head to the soles of your feet. It maps every synapse and molecule in your brain. Then it atomises you. It breaks you down into your component parts and sends these over to Mars, where another you is reconstructed to the exact same schematics using local ingredients. The question Parfit asked is: would the person on Mars be you?

Discussing this topic with my students and presenting it on social media, I noticed a peculiar phenomenon. People were okay with the idea of their brain being reproduced and with certain automatic cognitive functions – sweating, blinking and controlling our limbs. People were *not* okay with the idea that their memories would be the same. For some reason, people don't seem to like or accept the idea that all your memories are simply electrochemical transmitters and synaptic connections. It seems strange, reductionist even, to say that the last memory of your now-gone mother or the memory of the first time your daughter rode a bike is simply the high-frequency stimulation of neurons in your cerebral cortex.

But that's what a memory is, according to one of the pioneers in the neurobiology of learning, Eric Kandel.

In 2000, Kandel won the Nobel Prize in physiology for his work on the sea slug *Aplysia*. Kandel spent months gently touching the slug in different degrees to elicit or suppress the slug's protective reflex. He was teaching the slug to either grow accustomed to or be afraid of his touch. When Kandel examined the slug's nervous system, he found both new and altered neurons, suggesting that learning changes our neurobiology.

With a great evolutionary jump from slugs to humans, Kandel went on to prove that the signals we receive from our environment – our conditioning or learning experiences – do alter the structure of synapses. But there's a difference in how that happens. For *short-term* memory, there is a strengthening of existing synapses. For *long-term* memory, we create new synapses. In slightly technical language, short-term memory involves 'transient modifications in synaptic efficiency', while long-term memory requires new protein synthesis and the growth of new synaptic connections.

We still don't fully understand the neuroscience of memory, but we're getting closer. As more and more people suffer with memory-related disorders such as Alzheimer's disease and post-traumatic stress disorder (PTSD), learning the underlying neuropathologies of memory loss becomes more urgent. But, of course, there are sinister science fiction worlds lurking ahead too. If a memory is simply a synapse, a protein and a neurotransmitter, then we can reproduce it. It's not unreasonable to believe that in the next fifty years we will be able to entirely erase or create whatever memories we want.

Everyday Psychology
The Neurological Tale of Hannah and Tom

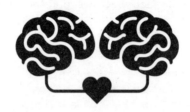

Roughly a hundred years ago, Sigmund Freud (see pages 14–15) gave us his division of the psyche. For Freud, our minds are divided into the ego (your conscious workstation in your head), the superego (moral norms and social checks) and the id (your bodily needs). The three are in a constant dance, more Argentinian tango than ballet. One of the most powerful, and often repressed, of the three is the id. Freud paints this as a kind of primal pull. It's eros in the classical sense – passion, drive, verve and, of course, libido.

Freud is often criticised for his lack of scientific rigour, but modern science now thinks he might be right about his id. It might not be a psychic energy or psychodynamic force, but our sexual drive *is* primal. Physical attraction occurs in a part of your brain that developed much earlier – the 'lizard brain', which is nearer your stem. So, what happens in your brain when you fall in love?

Here's Hannah on her way to a date. She has an elevated heart rate and her blood is run through with enough adrenaline to give her an edgy, twitchy kind of energy. She meets Tom, who is tall, handsome and very sexy. And so her brain pumps out dopamine, the reward hormone. Her body is flooded with: 'Go on, girl, do it!' As the date goes on and things are looking good, oxytocin joins in the fun. It makes her feel safe, comfortable and a little bit clingy. The rational part of her prefrontal cortex is trying to tell her to slow down. But oxytocin doesn't care. In fact, when we're in the early stages of romantic love, the brain regions linked with decision-making and planning ahead shut down. The primal shouts, and the rational cowers. Id over superego.

The date's a success, and after some behind-the-scenes fun, Hannah has an orgasm. Now oxytocin pulls off the gloves. Hannah's saturated with the nesting hormone. She's cuddly, snuggly and can't stop smiling. She's planning their wedding. The world is full of rainbows.

Over the weeks and months, Hannah and Tom become a couple. The dopamine and oxytocin are still there, but softer and less intense. They're building neural pathways; their brains are laying down roots (see pages 160–1). They get married and stay happily married for years and years. Somewhere between the orgasm and the grandkids, three things change. First, Hannah is more empathetic (see page 173). She can understand and care for others more easily. Second, she can control her emotions better. She knows when to get angry and when not to sweat the small stuff. Third, she learns 'positive illusions'. This is the ability we have to unconsciously or consciously overlook a partner's faults.

'Yes, he snores, but he's my Tom, and I love him,' she says as she gets into bed.

Olds and Milner
You're a Neurochemical Junkie

Your brain patronises you a lot. Whenever you do something your brain approves of, it will give you a little chemical pat on the back. 'Well done, Jonny,' my brain says, 'you ate some food. Here, have a bit of dopamine.'

Imagine you are an artificial general intelligence from the year 2026 and you're looking at *Homo sapiens*. What you will see is a featherless biped walking around in sad need of a hit. We're hormonal junkies, eating, drinking, working out, walking in nature – all because we want the next morsel of reward our brain deigns to give to us. To this AGI, we're not the apex species in touch with the divine, we're just rats who don't know they're in a maze.

One of the biggest steps towards this neuroscientific perspective of the brain came in the 1950s, when James Olds and Peter Milner discovered 'pleasure centres'.

Olds and Milner put brain stimulators onto various rats that, when activated, would release a surge of dopamine. In other words, at a press of the button, the rats would be flooded with the pleasure hormone. Olds and Milner then let the rats take control of their own dopamine release, in that the rats could press a lever to activate the electrode sites on their brains.

Of course, the rats pressed it all the time, little rodent junkies tap-tap-tapping to get all the pleasure they could. In the original 1956 paper, the team even noted that 'a hungry rat often ignored available food in favour of the pleasure of stimulating itself electrically'. The rats wouldn't eat or sleep if it meant they could press that button a bit more.

There are two facts to take away from this. The first is that we have a part of our brain specifically designed to give us pleasure. Over the years, neuroscience has concluded it's much more complicated and diffuse than they knew in the 1950s, but the general idea holds up. The second fact, though, is that animals will often do whatever they can to get pleasure, even if it seems contrary to their survival. A rat will press the button as it's starving. A human will play on their phone as the world burns around them.

For all that, we shouldn't extrapolate too far. Yes, rats behaved like zombies in need of a thrill, but humans are, at least sometimes, more complicated than rats. Our brains are bigger and far more versatile. We have higher-order thinking (see pages 180–1) which allows us to veto or suppress our more basic urges. But that doesn't mean we are greater than our brains. Our brain is still pulling the hormonal strings. These higher-order urges are no less electrochemical than the pleasure response. The actions you take every second of your life are all in search of the biggest and best reward.

Wernicke

Blibbering Flumfiddles

As you read this sentence, your eyes are scanning across it in saccadic, micro-jerking movements. The tiny, precise muscles involved are controlled by the magnocellular tracking visual system of your brain. This area also decodes the individual letters and words (called graphemes) into their representative sounds (called phonemes). It rapidly transforms the squiggles that make up the word 'bee' into the sound for 'bee'.

Meanwhile, Wernicke's area is what enables you to understand the meaning of words. Your angular gyrus is working overtime to link the visual, auditory, syntactic (grammar) and semantic (meaning) information. And finally, you have to remember what happens at the beginning of this sentence, and you have to hold that information in your working memory – for so very long, up to the very end of the sentence – which uses your working memory functions, found in the prefrontal lobe. If this makes you frustrated, well, that's the amygdala.

We know a lot about how the brain reads words. We know both the neuroscientific aspects and the cognitive functions required. The story of Carl Wernicke is a great way to appreciate how incredible language is.

In the late nineteenth century, advances in neuroscience depended largely on studying brain damage or mental deficiencies. With little in the way of cranial mapping or even surgical ability, it was largely impossible to perform any kind of open-brain surgery without killing the patient. So, psychologists depended on accidents and birth defects to illuminate the brain's workings. In his language studies, Wernicke focused on a special kind of aphasia which caused people to construct normal-sounding sentences that were made up almost entirely of nonsense. They might say something like 'Blibbering flumfiddles jickery crinzly blonmpfish' – normal rhythm, fluency, and even grammatical-sounding, but gibberish.

Wernicke hypothesised that there is a very small part of the brain above your left ear which is responsible for giving meaning to the words we use. The fact that patients with Wernicke's aphasia were proficient in all other elements of speaking apart from meaning implied that language was not confined to one area of the brain but was rather an emergent skill from the collaboration of many other brain processes.

Today, we know that no single part of the brain is usually responsible for any one thing, and Wernicke's area is only part of the language puzzle. The modern view is that our understanding of language – both written and verbal – is a kind of repurposing of other pattern recognition functions, like recognising faces or seeing rabbits in clouds. But Wernicke's area is still seen as essential to that.

So, as you read this sentence, give your brain a little pat above and behind your left ear. Thanks, Wernicke's area!

Penfield

Your Cranial Homunculus

There is a person on a table surrounded by attendants, ready to assist with his slightest need. Which sounds perfectly pleasant, were it not for the fact that this person is an epileptic with their skull cut open. It's the 1930s, and the Canadian-American neurosurgeon Wilder Penfield is performing open-brain surgery. Penfield has a small electrode probe that he is using to shock different parts of the brain. He's electrocuting this part and zapping that. Other than the local anaesthesia needed to remove part of the skull, the operation is performed with the patient entirely lucid. This is because, somewhat ironically, the brain itself doesn't have any pain receptors; it processes but does not feel pain. More importantly, though, Penfield needed his patients to be conscious to report on their sensations.

Penfield's 'Montreal procedure' was a first-of-its-kind open-brain surgery for patients with severe, life-deteriorating epilepsy. Penfield would stimulate parts of the brain with electric currents to determine what effect it had on the patient. A shock here, and a patient's arms would jump up. A shock there, and the patient said, 'Oh, I felt a tingling in my calf.' Through many of these procedures, Penfield developed a map of the brain. There is a photograph you can find online where Penfield has placed literal labels on parts of the brain – numbers to indicate which cortices did what. For example:

- 5. Numbness in the right side of the tongue

- 8. Felt sensation of movement in the thumb; no evidence of movement could be seen

- 17. Felt as if he were going to have an attack

That last entry was exactly what Penfield looking for. He wanted to identify damaged or scarred areas of the brain, with the goal of removing the problematic tissue. The Montreal procedure today has some impressive success in ameliorating the conditions of severe epileptics: most patients were entirely seizure-free after five years.

Penfield was brilliant, not only in developing an effective method of curing a debilitating disease but also in how he pushed the idea of brain mapping. Based on his research, Penfield developed a 'homunculus', a visual map of the various parts of the brain and how they affect our sensorimotor system.

Today, we are starting to see the not-so-science-fiction implications of what Penfield began. Now, there is hope for those with motor control issues, from epilepsy to Parkinson's disease, and even the possibility of 'neural implants', which allow us to control body parts – or even other external tools like prosthetic limbs – with technology placed in our brains. As always, though, science fiction has a dystopian side. Brain mapping of the sensorimotor systems also allows the possibility of literally controlling someone's actions: someone could be moved like a mannequin with a brain implant. As with any new technology, hope and fear are familiar bedfellows.

Everyday Psychology
You Make Me Happy

They were a couple once – a tightly knitted, loving marriage. In the late nineteenth century, the cracks started to appear. Philosophy wanted to get lost in linguistics and logic; psychology wanted something a bit more human, something relatable. The inevitable divorce in the twentieth century was more a drifting apart than a fiery break-up, and today, it's not uncommon for philosophy and psychology to be caught in the same bed; they will come together to shine their respective lights on the same topic. One of these topics is 'empathy'.

Where does empathy come from, and why is there such a variety of empaths in the world?

Nearly 400 years ago, the Scottish philosopher David Hume wrote that empathy was the 'propensity we have ... to receive by communication [the] inclinations and sentiments' of others. As Horace put it: 'the human countenance ... borrows smiles or tears from the human countenance.' Fast forward to now, and we call this 'emotional contagion' – the same idea, but in somewhat less poetic language.

Emotional contagion is when we witness someone else's emotions and start to feel a bit of them ourselves. If you spend enough time around someone who is embittered or depressed, then you start to reflect that back. Likewise, if you surround yourself with happy, smiling people, you'll find your mood starting to lift. This porous limbic system is down to our 'mirror neurons' – the parts of your brain that will act out what you're seeing or hearing without actually doing it. Let's say someone is telling you about getting into a fight. It's a dramatic tale of violence, injustice and thrown punches. Your mirror neurons will create similar feelings of outrage and aggression as the person telling the story. Mirror neurons are why we yawn when other people yawn, why we want to smile when someone else is smiling, why we feel sad when we see a crying stranger.

Why do we have this empathetic emotional contagion? What evolutionary reason is there for mirror neurons? We know that there must be some advantage to it because they've been recorded in many other intelligent animals, like rats and monkeys. In 2008, the primatologist Frans de Waal argued that empathy allows us to be more sensitive to our children's needs and so better at protecting their precious genes. Also, cooperation and 'altruism' serve as a tit-for-tat contract, where we hope we might one day be the beneficiaries when times are hard.

There is something a little depressing about the neurological and evolutionary explanations of empathy. It seems to reduce one of the few truly good things about humans to a game of 'save the genes'. But whatever the cause, we know that it's important, natural and near universal. It's what makes you laugh along with other people, and it's what makes a community happen.

Pavlov
Dog Spit and iPhones

You're sitting on a bench in the park, admiring some ducks. Such beautiful ducks. Then, someone shouts your name. You turn around and scan the area to see who called.

You pop into the supermarket, just to buy some milk. But then you smell the scent of freshly baked bread. You're salivating. You're hungry. You feel your willpower waning.

You're in the cinema and the lights go dark. Everyone hushes, then John Williams blares out over the Dolby surround sound. The *Star Wars* theme tune – you're a child again. You're lost in the anticipatory frisson of lightsabers, Jedi and lasers.

In each case, you've been conditioned. You're behaving like a dog.

Ivan Pavlov's experiments in classical conditioning are such a mainstay of popular culture that chances are you know about them already, be it via psychology GCSE, *The Simpsons* or from a chat in the pub. Pavlov rang bells when he gave food to his dogs. They salivated and gobbled it up. He did this over and over again. One day, Pavlov rang the bells without the food, and he found the dogs still salivated despite no food being present. That's the basics, but there's more to Pavlov than this.

Pavlov used his work on classical conditioning to work on phobias, habit formation and preference construction. He saw the capacity to self-condition and to condition others as keys to personal growth. When you boil down the essence of much self-help advice, you will often find the two mechanisms Pavlov identified: extinction and recovery.

Extinction is when you gradually weaken the connection between the conditioned stimulus (the sound of the bell ringing), the unconditioned stimulus (the food) and the response (salivation). So, ring the bell without the food, and the dog stops salivating. Or, if you turn your phone to greyscale, the reduced visual stimulation will supposedly lessen the dopamine hit, so you will check it less.

Recovery is where you reintroduce a previously extinguished response. Let's say you used to always listen to classical music as you studied. Over the years, Elgar has made you better at learning. But you soon find yourself listening to classical music before bed, and so it becomes more soporific than scholarly (an extinction). If you want to recover the original association, you have to limit classical music to study time. An addict who beat the habit by extinction will often relapse thanks to a 'recovery' of their conditioning, as when an ex-smoker goes through a time of stress, they 'recover' the connection between smoking and stress relief.

Pavlov is probably one of the most famous psychologists in this book. His experiments on dogs are easily repeatable throughout the pet-owning world. But not everyone likes what Pavlov's work implies. It implies that we are little more than dogs ourselves. We run to the sound of unseen bells.

LeDoux

A Spider in the Shower

You're having a shower. It's a long, Sunday-morning shower, warm, soapy and relaxing. You turn to reach for the conditioner and there, behind the bottle, is the biggest spider you've ever seen. You're pretty sure you don't get that-size spiders in this country. You yelp. You leap away. Or you freeze.

Let's pause this arachnophobic fun and zoom inside your brain. What's going on as you're cowering in a corner, screaming at foamy water? Well, the image of the spider goes into your eyes and up to your visual thalamus, somewhere in the middle of your brain. The visual cortex then passes the message onto your amygdala, right at the stem of your brain. It's here that things get interesting.

Your amygdala makes a judgement. It decides that this spider is a terrifying threat not only to well-nourished hair but also to your life. So, it tells your heart to get pumping. It tells your hormonal system to spike adrenaline. It tells your vocal cords to scream 'Arghh!' to try and scare the spider away.

According to the neuroscientist Joseph LeDoux, this is the 'low road' pathway of fear. It's the knee-jerk, automatic 'let's get out of here' response to a dangerous stimulus. It's what might save your life if you ever find yourself facing a mountain lion or an axe-wielding murderer.

This 'low road' pathway is contrasted with the much more cerebral 'high road' one. This is a less direct route, and therefore takes longer. This allows your rational, conscious voice to step in. Let's suppose that, after you've jumped out of the shower, your partner comes out from behind a door and says, 'Ha! April Fools!' and shows you the spider is a toy. Your high-road pathway will now correct the low road. 'Calm down, everyone; it was an annoying prank.' (Of course, if the existential threat turns out to be real, then the high-road pathway will confirm you are right to be frightened.)

LeDoux's two-path framework of fear is important in distinguishing types of emotional responses, especially between fear and anxiety. Sigmund Freud (see pages 14–15) argued that fear (*Furcht*) was just a short-lived response to a temporary stimulus. Anxiety (*Angst*) was worry, dread and background sense of unease. It's often untriggered.

Understanding fear is also a good way to understand the complexities of emotions more generally. The philosopher Rumi once described emotions as 'guests' in the 'house' of our heads. They come unbidden, unpack their suitcases and make the place theirs for a bit. This passive receptacle model fails to appreciate how far we can also create our own emotions. High-road reflection via the visual cortex can make us scared, even if there aren't any actual stimuli at all.

Educational Psychology

When I was a teacher, there was always a certain type of colleague, an educational archetype (see pages 134–5), who would say, 'Oh I don't bother with all that new research. Everything comes back around again.' Their point was that educational psychology goes in cycles. For example, 'learning styles' were all the rage last decade. Now they're out of fashion. But this section challenges my old colleagues. There really have been a few game-changing milestones in how we understand the learning mind.

Educational psychology is all about how we learn things and how to be better at it.

Bloom

Show Your Working

In Julia Donaldson's book *Zog*, we meet Madame Dragon, who runs a school for dragons to learn dragon things. They are taught to fly, breathe fire, fight and steal princesses. Over several years, they are taught all the skills needed by the fairy-tale villains they are to be. Each year, as Madame Dragon teaches her students, she returns to the same refrain:

'Now that you've been shown, you can practise on your own. You'll all be expert [at X] by the time you're fully grown.'

Donaldson's Madame Dragon has clearly been on a teacher-training INSET or two. And she's no doubt studied Benjamin Bloom.

In the 1950s, the educational psychologist Bloom categorised learning into a hierarchy. There are basic, and relatively easier, skills at the bottom and then higher-order proficiencies at the top. Let's use Zog to demonstrate what they are.

- *Knowledge*: This is the first step in any learning process. Zog has to know the skills involved in flying: how to beat his wings, how to hold his weight and so on.

- *Comprehension*: This is where the student recognises the reason for the knowledge. Zog learns that beating his wings creates a downward push, which lifts him up.

- *Application*: Practise, practise, practise. Zog goes away to try with all his might.

- *Analysis:* A student works out what is the most important part of the knowledge. They break down what's going on. Zog realises that he doesn't *need* to flap when he's in free fall, for instance.

- *Synthesis*: The skills learned so far can be used with other skills. Zog can combine flying with his knowledge of wind currents.

- *Evaluation*: A student can now critically appraise what they've learned, perhaps reinventing some of it. Zog learns to fly in his own way. He decides that jumping off a high cliff is easier than flapping, so he does that instead.

Ever since Bloom, curriculums have been designed in step with his taxonomy. 'Learning objectives' and assessment criteria are often weighted according to his hierarchy. Does a student demonstrate knowledge? Two points. Do they evaluate and critically apply that knowledge? Ten points! Well done.

Bloom's taxonomy has been revised, criticised and expanded since the 1950s, but it hasn't gone away. Proficiency is defined by skills, not knowledge. A first-year junior doctor might work, mostly, through the first three stages. A consultant brings in the last three. Expertise comes not from knowledge but from *applying* knowledge and knowing when.

I find the best way to explain Bloom's taxonomy is with a quote by the Irish rugby player Brian O'Driscoll: 'Knowledge is knowing that a tomato is a fruit; wisdom is not putting it in a fruit salad.'

Gardner
The Bird Competition

Long ago, when the rocks were young and the winds were new, the Nightingale, Peacock and Falcon gathered together to decide which one was best.

'Let us sing a beautiful song,' the Nightingale said, and – surprise, surprise – the Nightingale won.

'Let us flaunt our beautiful feathers,' the Peacock said, and – surprise, surprise – the Peacock won.

'Let us fly as fast as we can,' the Falcon said, and – surprise, surprise – the Falcon won.

'So, which of you is best?' the weary Owl sighed, and no one could tell him who.

In organic society, in your neighbourhood and on your street, you will find nightingales, peacocks and falcons. You will find different kinds of people who are good at different things. Because human society is diverse, no one is identical, and no two people will approach a problem in quite the same way. So when, for example, an employer seeks to hire only one type of person, they risk missing out on the benefits that others would bring.

Since the 1980s, the psychologist Howard Gardner has argued that we should stop talking about intelligence and start talking about *intelligences*. And we certainly shouldn't use IQ as the sole, unchallenged arbiter of smartness. After decades of studying development in both children and adults, Gardner concluded there are eight intelligences:

1. *Linguistic*: Those who work well with language. The smooth talkers and wordsmiths with a dictionary in their brains.

2. *Logical-mathematical*: Great at sudoku, probably likes chess, and does mental arithmetic for breakfast.

3. *Musical*: They can hold a note, tap out a beat, and rub their belly and pat their head.

4. *Bodily-kinaesthetic*: Dancers, athletes and yoga instructors.

5. *Spatial*: They know their way around a city and can navigate a space – surgeons need spatial skills, but so too do HGV drivers.

6. *Interpersonal*: Some people know if you're down, and they know what to say. They read people like signs.

7. *Intrapersonal*: Socrates at his best: 'Know thyself.' How am I feeling? What do I want?

8. *Naturalistic*: They know their poplars from their cedars, their honeysuckle from their jasmine. They're Charles Darwin with muddy hands and a magnifying glass.

The point Gardner is keen to stress is that no one is the same, and no one is ever good at just one or the other thing. We all have degrees of each type of intelligence, and every educational and industrial organisation needs to respect, nurture and work with these eight. Ultimately, no one is 'more intelligent' than anyone else.

Rosenthal and Jacobson

Superhero Poses in the Mirror

The author and historian Cyril Parkinson has a law named after him. It states: 'Work expands so as to fill the time available for its completion.' If you have a task due tomorrow, you'll get it done today, but not if it's due next week. If you have an essay to do, it can take you a week or a month, depending on the deadline. The job fills the space given it.

It turns out the same is true for people. When we have high (or low) expectations of someone, they will rise or sink to meet them. This phenomenon is known as the Pygmalion effect (and its corollary, the Golem effect). It shows the huge impact of expectations.

Pygmalion was a sculptor in Greek mythology who made a statue so beautiful and perfect that he fell in love with it. As the infatuated Pygmalion was also an attentive acolyte of Aphrodite, the goddess turned his statue into a real woman. Pygmalion married his statue, and they lived happily ever after in a story of dubious moral sentiment.

In the 1960s, psychologists Robert Rosenthal and Lenore Jacobson used this term in their book *Pygmalion in the Classroom*. What their book argued, and their research proved, is that when teachers have certain expectations of students, it hugely influences their future results. A teacher's behaviour and perceptions can either elevate a student or diminish them. Because of this, educators will now develop strategies not only to establish high expectations but also for the student to internalise and identify with those expectations.

Of course, this goes way beyond classrooms. In everyday situations, people are much more likely to behave honestly, kindly or generously if they're perceived as being so. It's why the old cliché 'I'm not angry, I'm disappointed' actually carries such a sting – most people try incredibly hard to meet the expectations or trust others place in them.

The Pygmalion effect is also about self-perception. It's about *identifying* as intelligent, patient or kind. There is a magic to self-belief, and fortune favours not the brave but those who *see themselves* as brave. It works the other way, too. Self-loathing and negative thoughts perpetuate themselves. In my life as a teacher, one of the most common lines I heard from students was: 'I'm bad at maths. I'm not a maths person.' I bet you know someone who says that. It might be you. The result is that these people just don't try. They switch off.

Rosenthal and Jacobson's study contains one of the most important pieces of motivational wisdom in this book. It's about having high expectations of yourself and others. It's about doing the Superman pose in front of the mirror. We can each be as brilliant as we see ourselves to be.

Bruner
Let the Kids Play

Sara is a doctor by day and an amateur chef by night. But Sara doesn't like recipe books. She doesn't like to be told what to do. She's a 'throw it in and let's see' kind of cook. It hasn't always worked out. The onion mousse last month was vomit-inducing, and her beef bourguignon had absolutely no taste whatsoever, but now Sara is an excellent chef. She knows what flavour combinations work and what culinary methods get the best results. She's learned to cook from the ground up.

Gabriel had a midlife crisis two years ago. He quit his job in the city, sold his million-pound house and went to live off-grid in Iceland with no electricity. He couldn't speak the language and could barely start a fire. But he stayed in his Icelandic village, and he learned. Many of his neighbours could speak broken English, and together, over two years of drinks, food and wood-cutting, Gabriel became fluent. He never learned formal grammar. He still does not know exactly what *ógnvekjandi* means, but his language knowledge is now deep and confident.

Sara and Gabriel embody something known as 'discovery learning', and it's a key aspect of American psychologist Jerome Bruner's work.

According to Bruner, classical education makes two mistakes: first, it treats all students as generic drones. Every person is the same, and so what and how we teach will be the same. Second, it gives students the finished product. A history teacher says, 'These were the causes of the First World War,' or a science teacher says, 'This is what plants need to grow.'

Bruner's constructivist theory of education seeks to invert both of these.

To address the first, Bruner advocated for tailor-made support, where learning is scaffolded according to the learner's abilities. This 'spiral education' technique presents learning in a repetitive manner, where each repetition spirals up with more advanced learning and more complex skills. For example, in geography, first you introduce the vocabulary and concepts of weather patterns. The next year, you introduce the underlying mechanisms of weather patterns. The next year, you consider how weather patterns affect agriculture and urban development.

To avoid the second mistake, students ought to approach a topic by exploring it. They do independent research into the causes of the First World War, and they try to grow a plant on their own. Sara messes about in the kitchen, and Gabriel stutters his way around Icelandic. This kind of discovery learning fosters curiosity, increases motivation, and gives roots to a student's learning.

Bruner's theory encourages us to embrace the journey of learning as much as the destination. When you next want to learn something, think about using discovery learning. Dive in with curiosity and a willingness to make mistakes. Allow your experiences and discoveries to guide you.

Thorndike
Find the Instrument You Like

When I was eleven years old, I had to learn the piano. I can't remember if it was a passing whim of mine that my parents took seriously or just something they wanted me to do, but for two years I sat resentfully through Mrs Upton's piano lessons. Mrs Upton was great. I just didn't want to be there. Three years later, bored in the phoneless days of the summer holiday, I picked up my dad's guitar. I learned three chords and sang 'Wild Thing' for six weeks. I sometimes feel sorry for my parents, but we can write it off as payback for the piano lessons. I loved and still love the guitar.

The point is that I wasn't *ready* to learn the piano. And, for the psychologist Edward Thorndike, who conducted some of the earliest studies in educational psychology, that's one of the three 'laws of learning'.

In the late nineteenth century, Thorndike put hungry cats in a box where they could see food outside. They were given various buttons by which to open the box and so get the food. Most of them were dummy buttons – only one worked. When the cat found the right button and was rewarded with the food, Thorndike would put them back into the box again afterwards to see if they had 'learned' which one was the opening button. From his various studies, Thorndike noted three common factors necessary to the fastest learning:

First, the *law of readiness*. As we will see on pages 212–13, one of the key factors in motivation is seeing the purpose of doing something. You have to want what it gives you. Thorndike's experiments involved hungry cats wanting food. They were ready. But scowling students in a maths class who don't see the point in trigonometry are not ready to learn. Thorndike noted that those who aren't ready *can* learn some things, but it'll be less efficient and slower than for those who are sitting at the front, back straight, pencil out.

Second, the *law of exercise*. On pages 160–1 we looked at the power of repetition – neurons that fire together, wire together. Before CAT scans and pithy rhyming soundbites, Thorndike noticed the same thing. The more you do a thing, the more competent you become.

Third, the *law of effort*. Two students bring their work to the teacher. The first is rewarded with a 'Well done! This is fantastic. Let's put it on the star worker's board!' The second is punished with a cursory look and a 'Looks pretty lazy to me'. Unsurprisingly, the first student will return to their learning cheerfully and with greater effort. The second will disengage and hate the subject. We all retain things better when we're given rewards – be that praise, a pay rise or cat food.

Dweck
You Can Be Better

If you've ever worked in a school or sat through your share of professional development courses, then I'm sorry. This section might trigger you a bit. Because if there is one idea that has come to represent corporate philosophy and educational cliché, it's these two words: 'growth mindset'. Growth mindset is our generation's 'positive mental attitude'. It's a pithy phrase people drop in to represent an important idea. But behind the slideshow presentations, poorly formatted handouts and guest speakers wearing 'listening faces' is an empirically supported, psychologically effective attitude towards life. It might not win friends and influence people, it might not make you richer and more attractive, but it might make you a bit happier.

The idea of a growth mindset goes back over thirty years to the American psychologist Carol Dweck and her colleagues. They were interested in what happened when people failed. They noticed that while there was a human tapestry's worth of variety, most people's reactions to failure fell into two camps. Some students were devastated, distraught and demoralised. They gave up, saying, 'Well, it's stupid anyway.' The other students shrugged their shoulders and got on with the task. The failure was a setback but the journey went on. What Dweck wanted to know was: what underlying beliefs motivated each behaviour?

Dweck coined the terms 'fixed' and 'growth' mindsets. A fixed mindset is one that says: 'This is who I am; this is what I'm good at; and that's not going to change.' It sees our skills and knowledge as innate gifts or curses. When someone says, 'Oh, I'm no good at languages,' or, 'People like me don't get to Yale,' that's a fixed mindset.

A growth mindset is one that fundamentally believes that we can all become better if we work hard enough at it. It is one that sees effort as the only necessary ingredient for doing or getting anything. You can become an expert in anything in 10,000 hours. A mountain's peak is ascendable one step at a time. You're not ignorant, you just haven't encountered that knowledge before. A growth mindset is one that has an unflinching faith in our ability to get better.

Dweck's research is correct. There are unignorable correlative associations between a growth mindset and positive attitudes towards failure. Growth mindset people often grow. The question becomes: how can we foster a growth mindset? And for that, I'll leave you with our guest speaker, Stanley McSmiley.

'Okay, everyone, get into groups.'

Zajonc

The Power of Being Watched

Anna is a runner. She's been training for six months for a 10km race. She's determined to beat her sister's personal best. Anna joined a running club, she read *Born to Run* five times and she even hired a trainer for a while. She's run the 10km a few times and come close, but she has never beaten her sister's time. The big day arrives. Her children are there with banners; her husband wafts a flag. The hooter hoots. Anna beats her sister's best time by minutes. It was easy.

Jonny is a writer, prone to distraction, and born with a weak will. Deadlines are distant problems, and if a job's worth doing, it's worth doing late. But one day, Jonny notices something. He works much better, and for much longer, in cafés. He can sit for hours, nursing a cold coffee and smearing his keyboard with lemon cake, when he goes to a coffee shop. The baristas glower, the manager pointedly walks by, but Jonny doesn't care; he's more productive here.

Jonny and Anna are two examples of a long-known phenomenon: we are all better at things when we are being watched. The presence of other people increases our arousal; it floods us with oxygen-rich blood and 'you can do it!' hormones. This was proven by the Polish-born American psychologist Robert Zajonc in the 1960s.

Zajonc's 'drive theory' states that when you are in the presence of other people, you will be stimulated and motivated to revert to your 'dominant response'. A dominant response is what you've been practising. It's the muscle memory and skills you've developed over the long, unseen hours back at home. A pianist practising for her Grade Five exam has been doing her scales and going over her repertoire for months. When she's in the presence of the examiner, she'll revert to this dominant response. What's interesting is that a similar effect is still noted if you *think* there is an audience (even if there may not be one). So if you think someone is watching you on a webcam, but actually they're off making a sandwich, you'll still enjoy the enhanced effect of being watched.

Of course, not everyone becomes fluid maestros on stage: some people clam up and choke. This is why the dominant response part is so important. Without the necessary habits (see page 161) or skills laid down in private, there's nothing for our body to revert to.

Zajonc's theory has interesting implications for educational policies, such as class sizes, presentations, group work and so on, but it's also a known phenomenon in moral situations. People who are watched, or feel watched, are often kinder and more ethical than those who act in secret. We're social beings, and it seems that being around people will often bring out the best in us.

Deci and Ryan
I Did It My Way

Have you ever done something just to spite someone? Or when you knew what people thought you were going to do, so you did the opposite? In his book *Notes from the Underground*, Fyodor Dostoevsky wrote that when presented with the 'beaten track' we're expected to walk, we will often 'stubbornly, wilfully, go off on another difficult, absurd way'. There's a part of us all that wants to take the untrampled path simply because it's different. We want to leave a mark that's ours, even if that mark is utterly detrimental or ridiculous. It's pig-headed and childish, but by heck, I'll do it if I want to.

Dostoevsky is one of the greatest writers of all time – not only a novelist but a philosopher, too. According to Edward L. Deci and Richard M. Ryan, he might also be a psychologist.

Deci and Ryan's 'self-determination theory' (SDT) suggests that all humans are motivated by the same three things: autonomy, competence and relatedness.

Autonomy is what Dostoevsky's talking about: we all like to feel like we're in charge. We've a primal need to assert ourselves on the world, and if presented with a life of deterministic, conditioned happiness, we'd choose anything else so long as it was our own choice. So, if an overbearing boss forcefully feeds their employees tasks without any consultation whatsoever, the employees will become disengaged and likely develop destructive behaviours.

Competence is the need we all have to feel effective. We want to be good but also to be told that we're good. On the outside, today's obsession with 'likes' on social media is a needy, narcissistic dystopia. But actually, it's just the modern version of seeking validation. A like is praise. A thumbs-up means we're doing well. It means we're competent.

Relatedness is about making meaningful connections with other human beings. It's about laughing and having fun, but it's also about duty and obligation. A parent gets out of bed at 2.40 a.m. to care for their vomiting child out of relatedness. A young man spends a month's salary on a stag-do weekend because those friends matter to him.

These three components make up 'intrinsic motivation' – the impulsion we have to do things on our own terms. But not all motivation is like this. Sometimes we do work because a boss tells us to. We slog at things we're not good at. We spend time with people we don't really like. These are all motivated by *extrinsic* factors, like the want of further reward (like a salary) or fear of punishment (like being fired).

The drive for autonomy, competence and relatedness often clashes with societal expectations and pressures. As we navigate the world's demands, there's a persistent, deeply human urge to assert our individuality, to choose our own path and to defy conventions. As Dostoevsky knew, we can only be *made* to do things for so long.

Kolb
What Could Have Gone Better?

When I was a teacher, it was common to give space for the students to 'reflect on their work'. Often, this meant the students would spend a few minutes after they got their essays back creating a list of the things that had gone well and the challenges they had. I would work my way around the room, checking in on what they wrote. Oh, the reflective gems I would read.

What went well? 'I got a good mark.' 'I wrote two pages.' 'I got it in on time.'

What could you do differently next time? 'Write more.' 'Get a better mark.' 'Revise harder.'

I'm pretty sure that teachers and students alike roll their eyes at the expression 'opportunity to reflect'. And it turns out it's heavily influenced by one man: American educational theorist David Kolb.

David Kolb's 'experiential learning theory' sees learning as a process where knowledge is the *transformation* of experience. According to Kolb, effective learning is a cyclical process of concrete experience, reflection, conceptualisation, and then experimentation.

Meet Archie, a history student. Archie has spent two weeks learning about the eighteenth-century British canal system, the watery backbone of the industrial revolution – hugely important, hugely boring. His 'concrete experience' was three hours of lessons with his teacher, a textbook chapter and a thirteen-minute YouTube video of dubious reputation. Archie wrote an essay and got feedback from his teacher. Now comes the 'reflection' part. His introduction was good, and his overall structure was sound, but he included some unusual assertions that seemed oddly tangential to his argument. In the 'conceptualisation' stage, Archie now writes what he will do next time: 'Don't go back to HistoryGeez1993's YouTube channel' and 'make points that connect to the argument'. Finally, Archie 'experiments' on his next essay and is chuffed with his considerable grade improvement.

What differentiates Kolb from other learning theorists (such as on pages 186–7 and 188–9) is his emphasis on the reflection and experimentation stage. Effective and *lasting* learning needs to engage different parts of our being; it needs to emotionally resonate, and we need it to 'sink in'. That only happens in the still moments of reflection and trying something new.

As annoying as it might be for time-stretched teachers and reluctant students, Kolb is right. Reflecting on our learning deepens it. Conceptualising mistakes and successes makes us improve much faster. Learning is not so much about repeating a fact or parroting a skill. It's about repeating the facts in a new context and performing a skill in *your* style. To do that, we have to experiment a bit. We have to take what works and ditch what doesn't. Archie has to get a bad grade before he can get a good one.

Bandura

Puff Kids Up

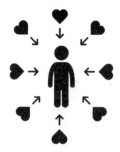

When Thomas Edison was a young boy, his teacher gave him a sealed envelope and instructed him to give it only to his mother. He did as he was told, and watched his mum well up as she read the letter.

'What does it say?' Thomas asked.

'It says you're a genius. The school isn't good enough for you. You're going to change the world.'

Thomas Edison went on to do just that. Even in his lifetime, the name 'Edison' became a shorthand for inventors and entrepreneurs the world over. Years later, when his mother died, he found that letter his teacher had given him. It read:

'Thomas is addled. He should stop coming to school. It's pointless.'

His mother, herself a former teacher, had read the letter and gone into a rage. She berated the teacher and took over her son's education. Thomas never knew. She showered him with love and praised his every achievement. His confidence and ability were not only due to her schooling but also to the self-belief his mother gave him.

Later in life, Edison admitted, 'My mother was the making of me.'

This (mostly true) story reveals something the Canadian-American psychologist Albert Bandura proved in the 1990s: the power of self-belief and self-efficacy.

Bandura's self-efficacy theory suggests that an individual's belief in their ability to succeed in specific situations plays a crucial role in how goals are approached, tasks are tackled and challenges are met. Self-efficacy is all about how much effort you're willing to put into something, but also how you tackle failure. It determines your motivation and resilience.

There is a cottage industry at the moment surrounding the notion of 'valuable failure'. This is all about the value of reframing setbacks as opportunities to learn and mistakes as essential for growth. Which is true. But also true is the fact that we need to have a certain degree of success in life to have the confidence to carry on. If we live life going from failure to failure (or have been told we're a failure; see pages 184–5 on Golem/Pygmalion), then, Bandura argues, we will be more likely to give up. In fact, we'll be less likely to start in the first place.

The story of Edison and Bandura is a lesson for all of us. We need to encourage and support each other. This isn't about a 'snowflake culture' of 'everyone wins!' races and safe spaces. This is about making someone strong and determined enough to withstand what life throws at them. A sapling caught alone in a storm will likely break. It needs nurturing and care to grow big enough to withstand the winds. We all need to learn self-efficacy, and that comes from inner confidence.

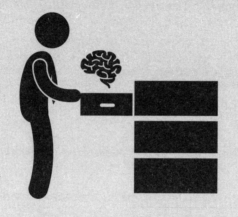

Occupational Psychology

If you spend any time around academics, you'll quickly realise that their job isn't really about tweed jackets, formal dinners and intellectual coffee breaks. It's about getting funding. Psychology is no different. All of the theories in this book are fascinating and offer great trivia to share, but a lot of them have very little monetary use. What's the cash value of social psychology? What's the point of spending ten years ringing bells for dogs? One area that doesn't lack funding is occupational psychology. It's the capitalist's research division, the money-making cousin that everyone else in the family both envies and resents.

Occupational psychology is how psychology applies to business, the economy and the workplace.

Maslow

Work to Live or Live to Work

Try to remember the last time you were nearly out of breath, or maybe the closest you've ever been to death. Was that the moment to scrub up your CV? Or to call your friend for a catch-up? A man on the gallows does not care how a novel ends.

These were things Abraham Maslow considered in his 'hierarchy of needs'.

In 1943, Maslow laid out his theory that humans have certain needs that are more important than others. He argued that our motivation to act is directed at the most pressing need. Someone suffocating looks only for air and won't care about an upcoming date. If you've got a gun pointed at you, you're not wondering how your hair looks. The greatest needs muscle out all the lower-order ones.

Maslow outlined five degrees of need:

1. *Physiological*: These are the basic biological functions needed to survive, like air, water or food.

2. *Safety*: This might be knowing you're safe from imminent danger, but also knowing that you're financially secure and healthy.

3. *Social belonging*: This means having a network of friends, family and intimate partners. A lack of these connections can contribute to mental health issues like depression, bereavement or loneliness.

4. *Self-esteem*: This manifests in both the need to be respected and admired by others and also as a 'higher' form in how we respect ourselves.

5. *Self-actualisation*: This is the existential creation of our identity. It's defining who we are and living our lives so we can fulfil our dreams and ambitions. It's the freedom to choose a path.

All these things matter. When we talk about 'finding a job you love', for instance, this assumes the job has met certain base needs. Colin might want to be an artist to actualise his creative identity, but he also needs to buy food and pay the rent. Erica might want more social events at work and praise from the bosses, but she also wants to know she won't lose her job next month.

Corporations and employees, both, often need to appreciate Maslow's point: 'self-discovery' or 'finding yourself' is hugely important to a fulfilled life, but it's often a luxury. Many people turn up to do their 9–5 just to collect a pay cheque. 'My work is like a family,' someone might say on LinkedIn. But for most people, their family is their family and they work because they simply need food on the table.

Herzberg
Why You Hate Your Job

It's that point in the conversation. You've done the hugs, you've all got drinks, and you've commented on how long it's been. So long. Too long. Now, you go through the tick sheet of pleasantries: 'How's your family doing?', 'Have you seen [a mutual friend] lately?', and the big, grown-up one, 'How's work at the moment?'

How's work at the moment? I'm glazing over just imagining the answers. Logically, there are only three: going well, going badly or 'Meh, it's a job'. What's more interesting than the latest in employee turnover in a company you've not heard of is the reason behind those answers. What factors connect the 'it's going well' people? What unites the work-haters?

This is what Frederick Herzberg's motivation-hygiene theory is all about.

Job satisfaction and job dissatisfaction are not caused by the same thing. In fact, according to Herzberg's theory, there are different factors behind each: 'motivation' for why people like their jobs and 'hygiene' for whether people hate (or tolerate) their jobs.

Hygiene, like its biological analogue, is about the bare minimum. Hygiene factors, when not present or poorly tailored, will make you hate your job; their presence does not necessarily make the job 'good' in the long term. They're just what you expect in a basic job and are often about the environment in which you work rather than the work itself. So, things like company policy on paid leave, how much supervision you get, what the workplace looks like, whether you're encouraged or allowed to talk to colleagues, and, of course, salary and security.

Motivation factors, though, are those parts of a job that genuinely make you buoyed to turn up. It might be the nature of the work itself – like if you're an accountant and you really like HMRC tax codes – but more often it's about the culture of the workplace. Are your achievements recognised and praised? Do you feel appreciated? Are you given opportunities to grow?

There are two interesting takeaways from Herzberg's model. The first is for employers and employees to recognise what exactly is bad about a job. If your dinner party guest says, 'Well, work's a bit crap,' you can use Herzberg to identify why. Or, if you're a CEO worried about retention, you can up your motivational game.

The other is the role of salary. Many people often equate salary with job satisfaction, but Herzberg calls that into question. The difference between a good job and a bad job is not more money. You can be hugely fulfilled and happy working for peanuts at a charity. Or you could be on a chauffeur-driven ride to a midlife crisis earning seven digits. The philosopher Hannah Arendt once argued that humans need to work to be happy, but work is not about just earning cash. It's about growing, contributing and adding value. Herzberg would agree.

McGregor
Good-for-nothing Workers

The evil wizard Sauron liked his orcs, but he didn't trust them. They might be good with an axe, good at eating hobbits, but the Dark Lord couldn't rely on them to look after a plastic cracker ring. And don't even get him started on the goblins. With workers like this, there was only one thing for it: surveillance. Constant, 24-7, sorcerous surveillance. He would make sure that his 'Eye of Sauron' could watch this feckless workforce until they got the job done.

Down the map a bit, a fellowship was gathering: Aragorn, the rightful king of everywhere, and his crew of noble elves, hairy dwarves and plucky hobbits. They all descended on Rivendell to contribute to the adventure in their own way, with their own skillset. This was a 'ask me anything' and 'all opinions welcome' kind of vibe.

Sauron and Aragorn represent two types of managers or bosses. According to Douglas McGregor, they represent Theory X and Theory Y kinds of mindsets.

Theory X thinking assumes employees are inherently lazy and require strict supervision. Workers are only in it for the money, and they'll cut every corner they can so long as they still get paid. Theory X is Dolores Umbridge believing the students at Hogwarts are always up to no good. It's Josiah Bounderby in *Hard Times*, who sees his factory workers as workshy drones who need a firm hand. It's that boss you had who wanted to know *exactly* what you did today. Theory X managers use a command-and-control approach, relying on rewards and punishments to motivate their employees.

Theory Y thinking suggests employees are self-motivated and thrive on responsibility. It assumes workers like or respect their role enough to do a decent job of it and to put in their best effort. Theory Y managers will say, 'My office is like my family.' They write work-loving LinkedIn posts and seem to actually mean it. A lot of tech companies will allow their employees to work on side projects – Google gives employees 20 per cent of their employment hours to work on their own things. The idea is that employees can be trusted to work on things that will be good for Google (Google's Gmail was born of this 20 per cent rule).

The difference between Theory X and Theory Y lies partly in how you view work generally. If you think humans have jobs only to fuel their leisure – 'work to live' – then you will be Theory X. If you think labour is inherently fulfilling, you will be Theory Y. But it also depends on the specific work. The drudgery of a Dickensian factory lends itself to Theory X, but creative, charity or purpose-driven employment allows you to work for the greater good.

So, which theory do you adopt? And is your boss a Sauron or an Aragorn?

Lewin

Good Things Come in Threes

There are two ways to make a bestselling book, movie or product. You have to come up with an idea no one has ever thought of, or you have to repackage an old idea in a new and exciting way. J. R. R. Tolkien didn't invent dragons, but he achieved huge success by taking them mainstream. Disney didn't write *Hamlet*, but *The Lion King* sure does make it interesting for kids. The same thing is true in psychology. Sometimes, someone comes up with a theory that isn't new but is repackaged to make it easier to digest.

This is the case with Kurt Lewin's 'change management' model.

In the 1940s, Joseph Campbell, the American literature and mythology professor, noticed that all the stories humans tell have three major acts: separation (in *The Lord of the Rings*, this is Frodo leaving the Shire), initiation (defeating Sauron) and return (cleansing the Shire).

That's the great idea, and Lewin (unknowingly) repackaged it in 1951 and applied it to industry. Lewin studied both governmental bureaucracies and business environments and noted the three steps that are common to all successful organisational change:

First, *the unfreezing*. You need to dismantle the old ways and tear down a few sacred icons. If you want to change, you're going to have to destroy the way things are. Psychologically, this is about mindset. You might need to abandon the old targets, philosophy or mission statement. Practically, this might mean moving offices, changing suppliers and firing certain obstinate staff members. To build it up, first tear it down.

Second, *the change*. This is when you bring in original strategy and new directions. You bring in fresh faces with new ideas. You probably spend a lot of money on making a new logo. In the dusty flux of demolition, you get busy.

Finally, *the refreeze* – where we stick with the new ways and consolidate. In some ways, the previous two steps are easy. You can destroy in minutes what it took years to build. The hard part is rebuilding, and refreezing is the hardest part to get right. When you return chaos back to order, it's hard to reestablish order. You have to reform good habits and have a cooling-off period. Change is not forever; you need to make the new norm the norm.

One of the more overlooked aspects of Lewin's work is the need to be psychologically prepared for change. Each step puts a great emotional burden on an organisation. It's exhausting and painful work to fire anyone or to say goodbye to the good old days. It's stressful to spend any long period in the change stage – humans, generally, like structure and boundaries. And finally, the refreeze demands effort and tedious repetition. Lewin's advice is that if you want to really make a change in life, be prepared for a hard job of it.

Hofstede
We Don't Do That Around Here

One of the sadder things about the streaming age is the loss of good adverts. One that's really stuck with me is an HSBC commercial from the 2000s. An Englishman sits at a table of Chinese businessmen, and he's served eels. He doesn't like eels, but in British culture it's impolite not to finish your plate. So he struggles his way through them. In Chinese culture, though, finishing your plate is a sign that you're questioning your host's generosity. So the Chinese businessmen quickly produce another eel to eat. The advert ends: 'We never underestimate the importance of local knowledge.'

It's a great advert because our cultures really do permeate everything we do, from dinner-table etiquette to philosophical values. It's these 'cultural dimensions' that concerned Geert Hofstede.

Hofstede's research in the 1980s looked at IBM, a huge company (like HSBC) that employed tens of thousands of people across fifty countries. Based on his observations and IBM's internal questionaries, Hofstede identified six different cultural dimensions (the examples here are his own).

- *Power distance*: How far does a culture expect power to be distributed? Latin American and Asian countries tend to value hierarchy, but Germanic and Anglophone cultures have a more egalitarian power division.

- *Individualism vs. collectivism*: Does individual autonomy matter more than group harmony? The Chinese tend to be more community-minded. The Western world tends to concern itself more with individual rights and freedom.

- *Masculinity vs. femininity*: Some societies, like Japan, emphasise 'masculine' virtues like achievement, assertiveness and material reward. 'Feminine' societies, such as the Nordic countries, will prioritise cooperation, modesty and caring for the weak.

- *Uncertainty avoidance*: Cultures with high uncertainty avoidance, like Germany, tend to have strict rules and regulations, while others, like Sweden and Denmark, are more tolerant of ambiguity.

- *Long-term vs. short-term orientation*: Does a country respect perseverance and long-termism or immediate gratification? East Asian countries, like South Korea and Japan, tend to have a high long-term orientation, while in Western countries we want things immediately.

- *Indulgence vs. restraint*: Frugal or profligate? Epicurean or Spartan? Indulgent societies, like Italy, focus on individual wellbeing and personal freedom, while restrained societies, such as many east Asian and Eastern European countries, prioritise self-control and patience.

I can already imagine the chorus of angry readers shouting, 'That doesn't apply to me!' And it's true that Hofstede's six dimensions do generalise, but they're still not far wrong. In 2010, a meta-study by Taras et al. looked at nearly 600 studies into cultural diversity and found '[Hofstede's] cultural values can predict certain organisational and employee outcomes similar to, or even stronger than, other individual differences such as personality traits'.

Your culture really does matter: never underestimate the importance of local knowledge.

Vroom

Why Won't You Tidy Your Garage?

When the Greek gods cursed Sisyphus for some hubristic slight, they had him push a boulder up a hill, only for it to fall straight to the bottom when he finally got it to the top. The torture was not so much the blistery ordeal of pushing a huge rock but that moment at the top of the hill as you watch all your work roll to the bottom.

We all like to feel that what we do *matters*. And this fact forms the basis of the Canadian psychologist Victor Vroom's expectancy theory of motivation.

Have you ever wondered why it is that you'll jump excitedly into some things but procrastinate over and delay others? If someone at work gives you a task, does it bump the rest down or go to the bottom of your list? For Vroom, there are three factors which determine that question: expectancy, instrumentality and valences.

First, we have to believe there is a correlation between our effort and some kind of performance. We have to *expect* that our hard work will achieve something. Second, we have to believe that this 'something' secures some kind of additional outcome. Third, and arguably most importantly, we have to value that outcome. We have to see it as worthwhile in some way.

Let's plug Harriet into Vroom's theory. Harriet is a first-year accountant at Big Money Inc. in the city. Harriet is hyper-motivated in her job because:

- Harriet believes that if she puts in extra hours to understand the latest tax legislation and applies this knowledge to her clients' accounts, her performance will improve.

- Harriet believes that her improved performance will be noticed by her supervisors and lead to a positive outcome, such as a promotion or a bonus.

- Harriet values the financial rewards because they enable her to support her hope to buy a house and save for the future. She values a promotion for future job prospects.

Vroom's theory of motivation was first presented in the 1960s, based mostly on theory and anecdotal studies. Since then, it's been proven over and over in various settings, from primary school classrooms to the corridors of governmental power. And it also applies to you. If you find yourself feeling lacklustre about doing something – you keep putting off a chore or hiding from a job – ask yourself which of the three factors is missing. Do you not see the positive outcome of tidying your garage? Do you simply not value sending Christmas cards to family you've not seen for three years? Motivation is not a divinely gifted boon. It's the result of underlying beliefs and background causes. Change those, and you'll be motivated to do anything.

Everyday Psychology
I'm Not Paying for Postage!

You're on the sofa, half watching TV, and you're shopping on your phone. You clicked on an ad, liked what you saw, and here you are, with a £200 basket full of jeans and shoes. Then you click 'Go to checkout'. Under your would-be purchases, slightly hidden, is the postage and packing line.

'£4.99?' you shout, and your partner jumps. You angrily close your browser, disgusted that any retailer in this day and age would charge you to buy from their shop. ASOS would never do that to you.

But, of course, ASOS is. You see, the people at ASOS have clearly read their Dan Ariely, and they know that if they add the delivery cost to the price of the clothes they can offer 'free postage'. And no more angry, empty baskets.

This example is known as the 'cost of zero cost', and it features in Ariely's book *Predictably Irrational*. For the book, not only did Ariely only call upon the vast library of literature out there but he also did his own 'undercover' research. He snuck into a dormitory at MIT to deposit a crate of Coke in a fridge. Within 72 hours, all the Coke was gone. He did the same thing with dollar bills, and after the same time, he found not a single one had been stolen. People are more comfortable stealing things than cold, hard cash.

Predictably Irrational challenges the notion that buyers make informed decisions. Instead, there's a kaleidoscope of underlying biases and hidden habits that influence people to spend a certain way.

Consider also the 'deadline paradox'. This is the fact that if you self-set a specific target, like 'I am going to run 5km on 17 May', you are more likely to succeed and be more consistent in your training than if you say, 'I'm going to run 5km sometime this year.' Then there's the 'relativity illusion', where people are more likely to make efforts to save on smaller purchases than large ones. When you move house or pay for a wedding, everything is ridiculously expensive. And so most couples don't think much about paying £2,000 for catering, even though there's a £1,950 option available. But if that same couple were out shopping for a new suitcase, there's a big difference between spending £100 and £50.

This is not just about marketing tricks; there's a wider point to be made. Ariely's work highlights just how susceptible our minds are to framing and manipulation. Understanding these biases and the forces that steer us can empower us to make more informed choices, recognise when we're being irrationally swayed and, if we're so inclined, perhaps even harness them for our benefit. Knowing the enemy is the first step to combatting it.

Adams

I'm Better than That Guy

$3 + 3 = 2$

Freya is furious. She's been working at APT Tork Inc. for five years. Even accounting for bias, she knows she's one of the most productive members of the team. She works herself silly for this company. The reason she's furious is because, over Friday drinks, the new guy, José, told her his salary. José is three years younger than her, from an entirely different industry and didn't even study the right thing at university. He's earning considerably more than Freya.

The reason Freya is angry at José is explained by John Stacey Adams's equity theory.

Adams's work starts with an observation about human nature and applies this to the workplace. The observation is that those born into the West have a fundamental sense of equity. We're motivated by a sense of fairness in how we view exchange relationships. We want to feel as if we're getting as much as we give. In our friendships, if we feel we're always the ones making the effort, then resentment starts to build.

In the workplace, this sense of equity is defined in terms of 'inputs' and 'outcomes'. Inputs are what you put into a relationship or a workplace – hours of work, years of experience, educational qualifications. But it can also be age, beauty or social status. Outcomes are the returns we get for our input – usually salary and promotion, but it could also be prestige and recognition.

So, Freya is furious because she perceives her inputs – productivity, effort, age and qualifications – are being unfairly compensated in comparison to José. Freya's case is an exaggerated one, but Adams's work highlights the micro-dynamics that underpin office politics all over the world. Kyle might resent his new boss, Eva, because Eva is half his age. It manifests in passive-aggressive putdowns and public sniping. Aria might hate Konrad because Konrad is earning three times her salary, and he hasn't even got a degree, let alone one from Oxford.

What happens, then, when someone perceives that their inputs are unfairly matched with outcomes? In his original paper, Adams lists eight potential behaviours. They might decrease their inputs – Freya might start working fewer hours – or they might leave the organisation. Sometimes, there might be some kind of cognitive dissonance (see pages 58–9) at play, where the worker pretends everything is all right. They distort reality to make it seem like their job is equitable: 'Oh, José must be doing more behind the scenes I can't see.'

Adams's equity theory is widely accepted in organisational psychology and has broad applications in managing workplace dynamics, including salary structures, workload distribution and recognition programmes. It feeds into training managers to recognise and address equity issues, which is also critical for sustaining a motivated and engaged workforce.

Locke

How to Keep New Year's Resolutions

It's January, and you're back in the office. Everyone's swapping stories about festive family arguments and awful hangovers. After a while, the conversation shifts to New Year's resolutions. There's the usual chorus of 'Nah, not for me,' and Barry gives his annual chortler: 'My resolution is to not make resolutions.' But then Dawn and Neil step up.

'Oh yeah,' says Dawn, 'I'm going to read more books.'

'Good one,' says Neil. 'I'm finally going to lose some weight.'

They've got admirable ambition but the statistics don't look good. According to a 2019 YouGov poll, around half of all resolution-makers will have given up by March. Only 6 per cent last the year. Maybe Dawn and Neil will buck the trend, but according to the American psychologist Edwin Locke's goal-setting theory, it's unlikely.

In the 1960s, Locke wrote an article theorising that since certain traditional 'motivational tools' like giving someone money or setting a time limit do not improve performance in themselves, the true motivation for completing a goal must lie elsewhere. Locke suggested that 'specific and hard goals produce a higher level of output than a goal of "do your best"'. It was a good theory, but it lacked enough evidence to become established. To prove he was right, Locke needed the work of a colleague called Gary Latham.

In 1990, Locke and Latham put their ideas together and gave us five principles of effective goal-setting:

1. *Clarity*: Goals should be clearly defined and easily understood by all involved. 'Losing weight' is too vague. Neil needs to be specific.

2. *Challenge*: Goals should be difficult but attainable, providing a sense of achievement when met. If Dawn's resolution is to read one book this year, it might be doable but won't be worthy of a 'goal'.

3. *Commitment*: Everyone should be committed to the goals, with a shared understanding of their importance. Neil should get his friends and family on board, with healthy dinners, running buddies and 'Go Dad!' signs at the Saturday parkrun.

4. *Feedback*: Regular feedback should be given to help team members adjust their approach and stay on track. Dawn should join a book club where she can be rewarded for her reading.

5. *Task complexity*: Goals should be challenging but not overwhelming. Neil won't look like Brad Pitt in *Fight Club* by the summer but he might drop a waist size by next Christmas.

I feel bad for Locke and Latham. Their work was pioneering and brilliant. It should have transformed the private and public spheres, and made them millionaires. Unfortunately for them, they lost out to George T. Doran's far more mnemonic SMART criteria ('specific', 'measurable', 'achievable', 'relevant', 'time-bound'). But whether you like your goal-setting à la Locke, Latham or Doran, the underlying principle is the same: not all goals are equal, and half the battle is in the setting of them.

McClelland
The Need to Achieve

You're at a friend's house and they get out a board game. How competitive are you? Would you call out your friend if they bent the rules?

Where do you see yourself in five years? With a better job title and more money? Or are you happy where you are?

You get a mark back from the teacher – it's 72 per cent. Do you think 'Well, that's good!' or 'Why didn't I get 100 per cent?'?

One recurring theme in psychology is the idea that humans are wired to respond positively to rewards. We are a goal-orientated species, and if we achieve a goal, we're happy. The interesting thing is that everyone has different goals.

For some people, the goal is greatness. I once knew someone who forensically studied the *Guinness Book of Records* because, as he said, 'There must be one thing in here I can beat.' He wanted to be top, and second place might as well be last place. Other people, though, are content with being contented. So long as things aren't broken, and everyone's as happy as can be, they will just cruise along with a smile.

According to David McClelland's 'need for achievement' theory, this latter group will be left behind when it comes to wealth, innovation and power.

In 1961, McClelland argued that people have various needs that they prioritise. For many, this is what he called nAch (need for achievement). People with an inflated nAch will set themselves high standards and strive to succeed. They will challenge themselves, and the moment they cross the finish line, they'll be looking for the next race. When you meet someone with an oversized nACH, they'll shake your hand, but you know they're sizing you up (see page 123). They're working out your weaknesses and trying to see how they're better than you. Life is a competition that nAch people need to win.

McClelland believed that higher levels of nAch will allow a society to experience faster rates of economic growth, companies to have greater entrepreneurial success and employees to be more satisfied in their jobs – but only in jobs with hierarchies to climb and promotions to gain. In short, nAch people have greater economic development, entrepreneurial activity and job performance. There's good evidence to prove McClelland right on all three counts.

Of course, not all people are nAch people. In fact, there's an argument to be made that a life obsessed with achievement can lead to burnout, stress and anxiety. So what are the alternatives? McClelland argued in his 'three needs' theory that other people need either power (nPow) or affiliation (nAff). Put together, that means everyone in the world wants either to win, to be in charge or to be liked.

Which would you rather be?

Goleman

Lonely Sandra, the Ineffective CEO

On Thursday nights, the Hare and Hounds pub is heaving with people: it's quiz night. All the tables are crowded, heads down and whispers only. In the corner, there is a table with one person. One woman, one drink, one pen. She comes every week and always sits on her own. One day, the landlord tells her tale.

'Oh well, that's old Sandra,' he says. 'She used to come with a big group. They always won. But she was mean. She ignored others' answers. She laughed at their suggestions. She banned any talk that wasn't strictly quiz-related.' He pauses to laugh. 'She didn't even let them hold the pen, by the end! One by one they left the team. Couldn't stand to be near Sandra. She never wins now, you know.'

The American psychologist Daniel Goleman could tell you what's going wrong here. Goleman argued that, more than any raw talent, more than IQ, the most important factor to effective leadership is *emotional* intelligence.

Daniel Goleman studied a lot of CEOs, and he noticed one thing common to the good ones. As he put it: 'The most effective leaders are alike in one crucial way: they all have a high degree of what has come to be known as emotional intelligence.' Good CEOs care about their teams. They have a highly sensitive sense of other. Today, a lot of people – especially those in the corporate world – know about emotional intelligence (EI). And, while the idea has been around since the 1960s, its popularity is mostly down to Goleman's 1995 bestseller *Emotional Intelligence*.

Emotional intelligence is about being able to read and interact with other people. Most people have some degree of EI. A small child seeing someone crying and thinking 'they must be sad' is entry-level empathy. As you get older, EI gets more complicated. It's about picking up on non-verbal cues and reading the unsaid. It's grading your language for your audience and changing topic if things are getting frosty. It's about social skills.

Being able to deal with other people is only half of the puzzle. Or, more accurately, it's 40 per cent of the puzzle. Because 'empathy' and 'social skills' are only two of Goleman's five components of EI. The others – 'self-awareness', 'self-regulation' and 'motivation' – are all about how well you know yourself. The deeper and arguably more important aspect of EI is to be able to know how you are feeling and to adapt your behaviour accordingly. 'I'm angry, I shouldn't send this email,' or, 'I slept badly last night; I'll probably do that job tomorrow.'

Emotional intelligence has transformed business and educational culture, and for good reason. Study after study has proven that leaders with high EI have more successful, motivated and happy teams. They win pub quizzes and are happy to do so.

Tuckman

The Fab Four and Company Retreats

No matter how desperately we try to avoid it, sometimes we all have to 'get into groups and do X'. Whether it be sports, a pub quiz, a community project or a task at work, we will weave our way through many groups in life. Some groups work, and some don't. Sometimes it's a kind of magical synergy, with creative and productive sparks flying all over the interactive white board. At other times, it's a name-calling, eye-rolling, sulky mess. So, what makes a good or bad group? What makes teamwork effective?

This is exactly what concerned the American Bruce Tuckman.

In 1965, based on several years of observing small group dynamics across a variety of sectors, Tuckman presented the four stages that every group goes through if it's to be effective. His theory was so successful that in 1977 he was invited to update his stages, and he did so by adding a fifth. For Tuckman, groups are a kind of evolving feature that need to mature and grow. According to Tuckman, they must pass through these five stages.

Imagine it's the early 1960s, and a group of young and good-looking men are picking up their instruments. They're making waves. They're playing the circuit in and around Liverpool, where quite a few of their audiences can be overheard saying, 'These Beatles are all right, aren't they?' This is the *forming stage*.

Their talent stretches across the Atlantic and the world, and differences start to bubble up. Paul liked strong melodies with a universal narrative appeal. John liked raw, emotional and edgier sounds. This is the *storming stage*.

Eventually, the two find a compromise, and The Beatles give the musical world *Rubber Soul*, *Revolver*, *Sgt. Pepper* and *Abbey Road*. A legend is cast in stone. Years of laughter, intimacy and friendship – the *norming stage*.

The Beatles are in cruising mode now. The media hang on their every word, and their posters decorate rooms from Portland to Perth. They tour the world with screaming fans, and they may or may not have been bigger than Jesus. They're into the *performing stage.*

Now the differences are too many, the personalities too big and the stress too much. The band break up. Everyone in the band has grown from their experience. John has a cult following. Paul is a national treasure. George has found religion. Ringo's learned to play the drums. They're all multimillionaires, and they're walking off into the sunset; they're walking into the *adjourning stage*.

Of course, Tuckman's stages of group development aren't unique to iconic bands; they're a blueprint for teamwork in everyday situations. When you're next starting an office project or joining a new sports team, ask what stage the group is in. Understanding and embracing these stages can turn even the most awkward, egotistical group into an effective team where members learn, grow and ultimately succeed together.

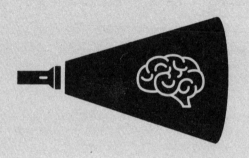

Forensic Psychology

Sherlock Holmes turns up on the scene to find a corpse, a murder weapon and feckless bobbies scratching their heads. 'Well, you can tell from the wound that he was hit from this side by a heavyset man who goes to the gym. The dandruff on his coat can't come from him – he's bald – so check that for DNA. He was clearly an addict, and he couldn't afford to keep it up.' Everyone is amazed. Sherlock takes his cheque. The killer is caught. Sherlock knew forensic psychology.

Forensic psychology is about criminal minds and criminal behaviour.

Yochelson and Samenow

Thinking Like a Criminal

It's difficult to imagine what it's like to have a criminal mind. Most people get angry occasionally: we've all tutted at a reckless driver or had a moan about a rude colleague. But most people wouldn't dream of then taking out a knife to stab the driver or a gun to shoot the colleague. It's hard to step inside a criminal's mindset because criminality is almost defined by deviancy. It's abnormal and antisocial. Even in the most lawless countries in the world, most people prefer not to break the law. Criminals are the way they are because they think differently to the rest of the general population. Sometimes this might be born of mental health problems or addiction, where criminality walks a very close line to insanity. At other times, though, criminals are just wired differently.

At least that's Samuel Yochelson and Stanton Samenow's theory of criminal personality.

Yochelson and Samenow spent fourteen years interviewing 255 criminals in various correctional facilities. They observed convicted criminals' behaviour and relied on the self-reported accounts coming from intense, years-long therapy sessions. Theirs was as deep and thorough as a longitudinal study can be into the criminal mind. In their study, the pair identified fifty-two thinking errors or fallacies that criminals tend to adopt. For example:

- 9. *Concrete thinking*: Criminals tend to see things in terms of black and white.

- 19. *Victim stance*: Criminals blame others for their actions; they are the victim.

- 25. *Ownership*: Criminals cannot accept that other people have things that they don't have.

And so on. The list is comprehensive and detailed, possibly *too* comprehensive. On a list of fifty-two beliefs or biases, we are all bound to score highly on at least a few. For example, being private and secretive (14. *Loner*) and feeling unique and different (11. *Uniqueness*) are fairly common. But, as Yochelson and Samenow themselves admitted, none of these traits alone will make you a criminal. Even all of them together won't make you a criminal. The list is a correlational one: criminals will almost always score highly on the majority. It's up to us – and law enforcement agencies – to consider how we use that information. Yochelson and Samenow argued that their list is best used in rehabilitation programmes where a thinking error is identified and addressed.

There's a deeper psychological point lurking behind what Yochelson and Samenow argued: the fact is that most criminals are not impulsive; they are often highly deliberative, and the vast majority of crimes are planned well ahead. Criminals reason and calculate as well as anyone, they just do so in a very different way from you and me.

Eysenck
Born to Crime

In 2011, the Los Angeles Police Department brought in Project LASER. LASER is an in-house algorithm-run computer system that crunches all the numbers and tells its user how likely X or Y is to commit a crime. Are you a member of a gang? That's five points. Have you ever been arrested for a violent crime? Five points. Have police officers ever spoken to you, formally or informally? Well, that's a point. Whirl, whizz, beep. Sorry, you're on the Chronic Offender Bulletin. Most police forces in most countries have something like LASER.

Criminal profiling and crime prediction are not new. Police might often keep an eye on serial recidivists, and even the *vigiles* of ancient Rome could predict that a big event at the Colosseum would require a large police presence. But Hans Eysenck's work on personality assessments was one of the biggest steps in criminal psychology of the twentieth century.

The terms 'introvert' and 'extrovert' go back at least to Carl Jung, and they're so widespread and commonly used today as to be close to meaningless. But when Eysenck used the terms in his theory of personality, he had a very specific definition. He thought that all humans have a need for stimulation.

We're looking to keep busy. In Eysenck's terms, we're looking for arousal (which in psychology only ever partially means sexual arousal). Eysenck hypothesised that introverts are more stimulated by the external world and more easily aroused, and so they are content to be more aloof or passive. Extroverts, though, are understimulated by life, so they need external excitement to top up their arousal.

Eysenck's work on introversion/extroversion and also neuroticism is interesting enough, but more interesting are the correlative observations he made about crime. Eysenck suggested that individuals with high levels of extroversion and neuroticism are more likely to engage in risk-taking and antisocial behaviour. Since they need to be stimulated, they push buttons and wind people up. Sometimes that toes the line of the law; other times it lands them in jail.

Of course, criminality is not something you can easily pin down. There are certain strong correlations – previous criminality, childhood abuse and so on – but very few personality traits that clearly predict lawless behaviour. In fact, criminal profiling is a hugely problematic and controversial area of forensic psychology. It's often swayed by underlying biases, usually racism, and it's easy to overestimate how much it can tell us. Criminal profiling can work and can be effective, but it's only one tool in law enforcement's belt. And, while we all like the idea of Sherlock Holmes solving a crime with a cursory glance at the suspect, profiling is only going to assist in an investigation; it can't ever solve a crime.

Raine
Insensitive Murderers

Your frontal cortex is the bit just behind your forehead. It's big, busy and important. The frontal cortex handles inhibitory control and decision-making. It's this part of the brain which tells you to not eat that extra piece of pizza. The bit which stops you from trying to sleep with anyone you find attractive. And stops you from punching someone annoying.

So, you'd expect that those who have an ineffective frontal cortex will be a bit more impulsive. They'll do things that might get them into trouble. And, in 1997, the psychologist Adrian Raine proved just that. The 1990s saw huge advancements in biomedical technology, and Raine was one of the first researchers to use the hottest new toy: the PET scan. A positron emission tomography (PET) scan works by detecting the radiation given off by a 'radiotracer' you have injected into your body. You can tell how well parts of the body are working by the levels of radiation they're emitting.

When Raine used his PET scan on convicted murderers, he found decreased brain activity in the frontal cortex. This was the beginning of a career that established the 'biosocial theory' of crime.

Here are some facts: people who are less sensitive and less reactive to the world are more likely to be murderers. Or, in more technical language, those with 'blunted autonomic functioning' are more likely to be criminals. For example, people with low resting heart rate and poor skin conductance are more likely to be psychopaths.

Those are facts. What do we do with them? The instinctive and tempting thing to do is to conclude that criminality can be explained by biological factors, and it's not unfair to suggest that Raine's work does lean into that perspective.

But Raine's biosocial theory is not so blunt or as simplistic as that. Biology is not fate, and we are not forced to live according to our genetics. People with blunted automatic functioning are more likely to be criminal, but that doesn't *make* them criminal. There are millions of people with low resting heart rates who aren't murderers.

Raine expanded the debate Eysenck (see pages 230–1) began: to what extent can criminality – or any behavioural tendency – be better explained by innate biology or by our socialisation? Is someone a criminal by nature or by nurture? As is almost always the case, the answer lies somewhere between the extremes, but Raine's view tends more towards biology. Aggression, psychopathy and low impulse control *do* have physiological explanations, and all overwhelmingly correlate with criminality.

All of which is to say, if you know someone with low heart rate, it's probably best not to get into a row with them.

Gottfredson and Hirschi
I Can't Help It

Have you ever given in to temptation and eaten too much ice cream? Well, you're probably going to be a criminal.

Have you ever said no to a gym session in order to sit on the sofa and watch TV? It won't be not long until you burgle someone's house.

Have you ever cheated on a partner? It's only a matter of time before you turn to murder.

Okay, I'm being sensationalist. I'm warping reputable science in the hunt for an exciting opener, but the basic premise behind these predictions lies at the centre of Michael R. Gottfredson and Travis Hirschi's 'general theory of crime'.

There is a difference between criminality and crime. Criminality is the propensity or willingness to commit a crime. In the right circumstances, and given the right cost–benefit analysis, a highly criminal person will commit a crime. For Gottfredson and Hirschi, a crime will only occur when someone with a certain degree of criminality meets the opportunity. But since these opportunities come up all the time, people with high levels of criminality will almost always, inevitably, commit a crime.

So, what determines your degree of criminality? For Gottfredson and Hirschi, it's about risk-seeking, thrill-seeking personalities. More than anything, though, it's down to low self-control. Your degree of self-control is partially genetic – impulse regulation predominantly occurs in the frontal cortex, and some people have stronger or better versions of this (see page 157). But according to Gottfredson and Hirschi's research, low self-control is more often caused by environmental influence.

Self-control develops early in life and is moulded by factors such as parental supervision, recognition of deviant behaviour, and appropriate responses to deviant behaviour. In other words, low self-control comes from when a child was either never told to stop doing a thing, never told a thing was wrong, or never punished for doing something wrong.

Gottfredson and Hirschi's general theory of crime is popular and has been reconfirmed by many psychologists since their original 1990 paper. But in 2006, a team from Florida Atlantic University criticised it for being tautological: a circular argument that simply states the obvious. They claimed that without defining 'low self-control', Gottfredson and Hirschi were essentially saying: 'People who break the law are people who often break the rules.' Well, yes. Those who don't stick to rules are not going to stick to them when they're written up in legal language.

All of which is to say that if you eat too much ice cream, you know what the consequences might be.

The McNaughton Rule
Legal Insanity

Daniel McNaughton was the son of a Scottish whittler. He believed there was a plot to kill him. McNaughton was adamant that Catholic priests from France were in league with the Tory government and were closing in. They had infiltrated England and were making their way up to Glasgow to murder him 'for crimes of which I am not guilty'.

McNaughton reported his delusions to the Commissioner of Police, but he was ignored. On 20 June 1843, McNaughton saw Edward Drummond, Sir Robert Peel's private secretary, leave the Prime Minister's house and shot him in the back five times. Drummond died. McNaughton had confused Drummond for Peel.

McNaughton was arrested, and the finest lawyers and physicians of the day congregated at the trial, a trial that would change criminal history. The defence counsel had the esteemed Dr Edward Monro from Bethlem Hospital confirm that McNaughton genuinely believed his delusions. Six other expert doctors testified that McNaughton was undoubtedly insane. McNaughton was acquitted of murder and was institutionalised for the rest of his life.

This case gave rise to the 'McNaughton rule' (sometimes 'M'Naghten'), the legal standard used to determine whether a defendant can be considered legally insane and therefore not responsible for their criminal actions.

The McNaughton rule sets two criteria for criminal insanity: the accused must either not know what they were doing or, if they did know what they were doing, they must not be able to differentiate between right and wrong.

So, imagine someone sitting calmly on the doorstep of his house, waiting to be arrested. He has just killed his entire family. At the trial, it becomes clear that he has no recollection whatsoever of what happened. The man would be declared criminally insane.

Or, imagine a schizophrenic who hallucinates someone in the supermarket is a scaly evil demon out to kill them. They take a bottle and smash it over the person's head. They *do* know what they are doing, but they do not think what they are doing – fighting off a demon – is wrong. She would be declared criminally insane, too.

The McNaughton rule has its criticisms – namely, that it doesn't align with psychiatric definitions of insanity, which often consider underlying neuro-pathologies rather than simply behaviours. Secondly, it fails to account for 'temporary' vs. structural insanity. A 'crime of passion' committed by someone who couldn't control their actions could be considered 'temporary insanity', yet they seem more morally culpable than someone with schizophrenic delusions.

The problem is that laws have to draw a line somewhere, and because mental health is a spectrum rather than binary, there is always going to be some detail lost. For all that, it's still the best rule we have.

Loftus and Palmer
My Childhood is a Lie

My mum will sporadically clean out her house. She's going through a decluttering phase at the moment. And when my mum declutters, I clutter. 'Hello, darling,' she will say, with the wide grin of the sadist. 'I've got five boxes here full of your childhood toys.'

Great!

Mum will pull things out and tell me how much I loved this bear or how I would never leave this toy alone. Mostly out of filial duty, I kept one of my most cherished bears – a hand puppet called Puppy.

Last Christmas, my brother came to stay. He looked at my beloved Puppy and said, 'Oh, you've got Gerry!'

'Who?'

'Gerry, you've got Gerry.'

It turns out that Puppy is actually Gerry. This isn't my most cherished bear at all. It's not even my bear. My mum has spun a yarn fit for a bard and is, right now, laughing all the way back to her immaculate house.

Philosophers and psychologists agree that our memories are essential to our sense of self. What we remember forms the bedrock of our personal identity. But fifty years ago, the psychologists Elizabeth Loftus and John Palmer revealed how malleable and fallible memories can be. Loftus and Palmer had forty-five participants watch footage of a car accident. They were then asked, 'How fast were the cars going when they [hit/smashed/collided/bumped/contacted] each other?'

What the interviews revealed was that the verb the questioner used significantly influenced participants' recall. Those hearing 'smashed' reported higher speeds and even said they saw broken glass, though there wasn't any in the footage. Loftus and Palmer challenged the common belief that memories are fixed. Instead, memory is shown to be a dynamic, reconstructive process that can be distorted and manipulated.

There are two big implications for this. First, in the legal sphere, it questions the reliability of convictions based heavily on eyewitness accounts. Lawyers, judges and lawmakers had to reappraise the notion of leading questions and the weight given to this kind of testimony. More broadly, though, it forces us to reconsider our own and others' memories. Your sense of self is built upon what you remember. Childhood birthdays, a first kiss and that time you won a race are foundational to who you are. What Loftus and Palmer showed is that you might be remembering a lie. Your self is a construction. Puppy is actually Gerry.

Everyday Psychology
Do Video Games Make People More Violent?

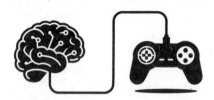

In 1997, a fourteen-year-old boy named Michael Carneal walked into Heath High School, Kentucky. He put in some earplugs, pulled a pistol from his bag, and started shooting. Carneal killed three girls and injured five others. He was sentenced to life in prison.

In the wake of the Kentucky shooting, the parents of the three murdered girls filed a lawsuit against the media industry worth $130 million. The prosecutors argued that Carneal was influenced by certain movies and violent video games like *Doom*, *Quake* and *Mortal Kombat*. The lawsuit failed, but the issue didn't go away. The 'violent games cause violent children' debate pops up in the media every generation. Games were blamed in Kentucky, but also in 1999 at Columbine, in 2007 at Virginia Tech, and in 2012 at Sandy Hook.

So is there any truth in the idea that playing violent games makes you more violent?

One of the reasons why the debate hasn't died is that it seems incredibly plausible. If you spend hours of your day killing hyper-realistic humans, shooting animals or punching strangers, surely that must affect you. One of the shooters at Columbine, Eric Harris, is reported to have said, 'I will force myself to believe that everyone is just another monster from *Doom*,' before the massacre. At the very least, it desensitises you to trauma and normalises violence. In 2000, the American psychologists Craig Anderson and Karen Dill had 210 students play either a violent game or a gentle one. They found that in the hours after playing the violent-game-playing students would demonstrate more violent behaviour when given a 'punish your opponents' activity.

The most recent evidence, though, casts doubt on how justified the moral panic might be. In 2016, Cunningham et al. studied whether exposure to violence primes you to violence in a real-world setting, not just in a laboratory experiment. The team concluded: 'We find no evidence of an increase in crime associated with video games and perhaps a decrease.' It was a conclusion that confirmed an earlier meta-study in 2008, where Ferguson et al. found the same thing. The studies went on to say that most people are quite capable of differentiating between 'real' and 'game', and the priming effects of saturating yourself with violence will only be short-lived.

The video game debate is not only complicated in itself but also reflects a wider issue in psychology: that of confounding factors. You cannot isolate two identical and otherwise blank human beings in order to give one a computer game and the other none. There is no control group or placebo possible here. A violent man might play violent games, but he might also have family problems, mental health issues, certain values and genetic propensities. Correlation does not equal causation, and with humans, there are a *lot* of factors that can muddy the waters.

Cleckley
Behind the Smile

On 19 July 2017, the wife of Chester Bennington – the lead singer of Linkin Park – shared a family photo. It was a happy scene of the Bennington family standing on a balcony, looking out at the sea. Chester is seen laughing and at ease. A happy dad and loving husband, living the dream. The next day, Chester took his own life. Behind the pretence was a man deeply ill. In the UK, suicide is the leading cause of death among men under fifty. It's almost entirely to do with traditional and toxic masculine expectations: keep it together; boys don't cry; never be a burden; asking for help is weakness. But behind the smiles and 'I'm fine' is something broken.

This observation goes back a very long time, and in the 1940s, the American psychiatrist Hervey Cleckley gave us the term 'the mask of sanity'.

In Cleckley's book of the same name, the mask of sanity describes the way individuals who are experiencing profound emotional trauma and interpersonal deficits can appear normal on the surface. Cleckley accepted that this 'mask' can apply to a raft of mental health conditions, such as depression or suicidal thoughts, but his work was mostly about psychopathy.

Decades before Robert Hare's psychopathy test (see page 245), Cleckley proposed sixteen criteria to identify psychopaths, like having superficial charm, a lack of remorse or guilt, and poor judgement. But more than being simply a diagnostic toolkit, Cleckley's work revealed how difficult it is to identify pathological mental conditions in those determined to hide them. Psychopaths *appear* normal. Depressives *appear* happy. Anxious people *seem* chilled.

The 'mask of sanity' highlights a real challenge in psychiatry today: how to diagnose conditions that involve appearances, not least the differentiation between sanity and psychopathy. Of course, the problem stretches into treatment as well. It's easy for someone to walk away from their psychiatrist saying, 'Thanks, doc, I'm all better now,' but feeling as troubled and unwell as before. At the end of his book, Cleckley asks, 'What can be done?' He not only believed his own efforts to treat psychopathy had failed, but he thought it was impossible to succeed. There's no easy metric to detect mental health conditions or measure their amelioration.

Today, things are better. Health professionals often employ a comprehensive assessment strategy for an of-concern patient that goes beyond traditional diagnostic criteria and considers the deeper, often hidden, aspects of an individual's psychological state, relying only partially on self-reported testimony.

But even this is not foolproof, and someone determined to hide their problems can often do so. The 'mask of sanity' idea does serve as a reminder to us all to look out for our loved ones. No one can pretend forever, and when a mask does slip, it's always worth a second look.

Hare

Why Your Ex is Almost Certainly Not a Psychopath

In the late nineteenth century, mental asylums were unregulated, shadowy vaults of misery and torture. Cold baths, forced starvation and regular beatings were not hidden anomalies, they were routine. And so, in 1887, the journalist Nellie Bly feigned insanity to go undercover to expose what happened at Blackwell's Island asylum in New York.

From almost the moment she arrived, Bly stopped pretending to be mad. She carried on her life as she would in the outside world. What was strange, though, was that the guards and attendants kept pathologising her behaviour. Everything she did was seen through the prism of madness. Her journalling was perceived as obsessive note-taking. Her talking to other inmates was a psychological tic. Even pleading for release was a symptom. After all, *everyone* on Blackwell's Island wanted to get out.

Bly's story, written in her book *Ten Days in a Mad-House*, revealed a troubling fact about many psychological tests: the tendency to confirmation bias.

In the 1990s, Dr Robert Hare gave us the psychopathy checklist. This is a semi-structured interview designed to test a subject against twenty specific traits associated with psychopathy. For instance:

- Is this person glib and have superficial charm?
- Do they have a sense of personal grandiosity?
- Do they need constant stimulation?
- Do they lie, manipulate and play games with people?
- Do they lack remorse and empathy?

When the Hare psychopathy test is done properly by trained psychologists who pay attention to the right metrics, it's hugely effective. It's used in academic literature, in high-security prisons and in courtrooms. The problem, though, is when people use it to self-diagnose or to diagnose the people in their lives.

'My ex is certainly a psychopath,' someone might say. 'He lied all the time. *Pathological* liar, he was.'

As Bly discovered, if you set out trying to find pathological behaviours, you will find them. Most people, most of the time, will test positive for *some* of the twenty psychopathic markers. That doesn't make them psychopaths. Mental health is a serious issue for many people and isn't to be diagnosed lightly. Armchair psychiatry is almost always wrong and harmful.

Capote
The Road to a Crime

We are living in an age of 'true crime'. If you dig out any Top Ten menu on Netflix, Amazon, Disney+ or wherever, you'll notice a scattering of true crime documentaries. There's something compelling about the 'non-fiction novel' – a story that is so well plotted and fleshed out that you can hardly accept it's real. While we live in the golden age of true crime, it's a genre that really took off eighty years ago with one of the most famous non-fiction books of all time: Truman Capote's *In Cold Blood*.

Most authors get pretty involved in their work. Agatha Christie and J. K. Rowling made book plans that looked more like nuclear reactor schematics. J. R. R. Tolkien invented an entire, grammatically appropriate language for his Middle Earth. But Capote got so far into his research that he not only created a genre but redefined what psychological analysis ought to look like for criminal investigations.

In Cold Blood is set, ostensibly, in Holcomb, a gentle community where everyone knows your name. A tranquil backdrop to four brutal and bloody murders. But the book doesn't stay in Holcomb for long. It unpacks and explores the lives of the eventual killers, Richard Hickock and Perry Smith. Over a series of vignettes and short chapters, the book works its way closer and closer to the Holcomb massacre, by which time we know Hickock and Smith like friends.

And Capote almost did call Smith a friend. Capote interviewed both killers, but he was especially captivated by Smith. He saw Smith as a gentle, sensitive soul who was brought to the murder almost by accident, via the unhappy path of his life. The reader, too, is left unsure of how to interpret Smith. He was obviously guilty, and yet he didn't seem as guilty as the much more cold-blooded Hickock. We all could have been Perry Smith if we had been dealt the same cards.

And it's this idea that Capote leaves to psychology. In humanising Smith, he calls attention to the fact that every criminal is made criminal not by some innate violent streak or lapsarian evil but by circumstances. Behind most murders lies a history of misery, abuse and hardship. When you know that history, you can empathise with, if not forgive, the criminal action. Especially for someone like Perry.

Capote's book is aimed not at justification but at understanding. It pieces together the fragments of a shattered mirror to glimpse the distorted reflections within. It allows us to appreciate the work of forensic psychologists, detectives and judicial bodies all the more – there is no such thing as evil, per se, and everything about human psychology is complicated.

Canter
The Mind of a Murderer

Here's a macabre but fun experiment you can try at home, when you next have a group of friends over. *Ask everyone how they would commit murder.* Ask for specifics. Where, when and with what? How would they plan to get away with it? Sit and listen in on the variety of homicidal fictions.

If David Canter is right, everyone in that room will have their own particular flourish for murder.

British psychologist Canter is one of the biggest names in psychological criminal profiling. Canter argues that the way someone commits a crime reflects their personality. Therefore, working backwards, if we know how a crime took place, then we can work out what specific behavioural patterns we're looking for in a suspect. This profiling involves carefully analysing the crime scene, examining the nature of the crime and any patterns that may indicate the offender's habits, lifestyle and possible psychological traits.

For instance, suppose there has been a spate of high-end burglaries. The culprit leaves no fingerprints, uses sophisticated tricks to bypass security systems and is careful to avoid leaving any DNA or evidence behind. The burglaries are done quickly and with precision, targeting specific valuable items while leaving other expensive but easily traceable items untouched. From this, we can discern that the criminal is intelligent, technologically savvy, meticulous and has some knowledge of the criminal world.

Of course, some form of criminal psychological profiling has been around as long as good policing. If a serial killer targets only black people, it's likely you're dealing with someone with racist beliefs. If someone is murdering only gay people, then they're likely homophobic. However, good Canter-style profiling can be more subtle. Ted Bundy, for instance, was one of the most notorious serial killers in American history. He lured, raped, tortured and killed more than thirty women all over the USA. He was captured at least partially thanks to psychological profiling. His need to torture suggested a desire for power and control. The fact he carried on killing implied he had some pathological need for thrills or adrenaline. The fact that his victims were almost always manoeuvred into his path implied he was charming, manipulative and charismatic.

Criminal psychological profiling works, but it can be problematic when not done well. As we saw on pages 134–5, stereotyping is often an essential part of being human, but it can also lead us to biases and fixations. If they rely too heavily on profiling, criminal agencies risk excluding anomalies or statistics that buck the trend. It's true that most fatal poisonings are committed by women, but that doesn't mean men can't use poison too.

Münsterberg

Leading Questions

Once upon a time, forty people were shown a picture of a farmer's room. It was a detailed and busy room. Researchers then asked a series of questions. How many people were in the room? Did the room have any windows? What was the man doing? In each case, the people answered correctly most of the time. But then the researchers started asking more detailed questions, like 'What colour was the stove?' and 'How many eggs were on the table?' What they discovered was that people would just invent answers. They would invent hundreds of new objects or pieces of information based on the suggestion of the question.

This was a real experiment described in the German-American psychologist Hugo Münsterberg's 1908 essay 'On the Witness Stand'. On page 239, I mentioned the famous Loftus and Palmer experiments involving eye-witness testimony of a car crash. Münsterberg was making the same point decades earlier.

Münsterberg's aim was not only to highlight the fallibility of testimony and memory recall, he was also trying to challenge the idea that lawyers and courts are objective, aways getting to the truth. A suspect can be steered to say certain things. A witness can be manipulated. An expert can be guided. This was at least partially known in 1908. A lawyer could object to a cross-examiner's question as 'leading' and have it struck from the record. But Münsterberg's showed that that suggestibility kicks in far more quickly than lawmakers realised. The other side might 'reject a too clumsy suggestion as an unallowed "leading question"' but almost all questions, unless very carefully scripted, will guide, manipulate and elicit a certain response.

Münsterberg also highlighted the possibility of false confessions. Like with suggestible memories, under the manipulative hand of a seasoned interrogator, a suspect can be made to say and confess to anything. As Münsterberg put it: 'The degree of suggestibility changes from man to man and changes in every individual from mood to mood, from hour to hour ... Even the most stubborn mind is open to certain suggestions ... Emotion certainly increases suggestibility with everybody; so does fatigue and nervous exhaustion.'

Most people in the civilised world oppose torture. Not only is it inhumane but it almost always leads to false or warped confessions. I would admit to being the Queen of Sheba if it meant I wasn't tortured, and I suspect you would, too. But you do not have to torture a person to make them say outlandish things. You have only to ask the right questions. Justice requires that we acknowledge the nuances of human suggestibility. As Münsterberg wrote: 'Suggestions are able to turn white into black and black into white; it seems indeed astonishing that the work of justice is carried out in the courts without ever consulting the psychologist.'

Everyday Psychology
Murder Voyeurs

True crime is not a modern phenomenon. If you stretch the definition to breaking point, you could even say it's as old as village gossip. 'Did you hear that they caught Ol' Jim for stealing?' But, as an identifiable genre, true crime needed two things: the printing press and the criminal justice system. Neither of which is especially new. In the sixteenth century, criminal reports were printed for the upper classes, and woodcut illustrations were made for the poor and illiterate. In seventeenth-century Britain, 'last good night' ballads were narrative reworkings of the speeches made by convicts before they were executed.

But the current market saturation of true crime *is* a new thing. From 2014's *Serial* podcast to Netflix's record-breaking ratings for *Tiger King* in the 2020 lockdown, it's fair to say the world loves a good true crime drama. What can this obsession tell us about the human psyche?

Here is a series of seemingly dissonant facts. Women are overwhelmingly the victims in true crime documentaries. Women are more disgusted than men by gory experiences like touching a cadaver. And yet, women also enjoy true crime documentaries twice as much as men.

In 2021, a paper from Illinois Wesleyan University interviewed thousands of women about their true crime habits and found a few common threads. First, women are much more likely to be scared in encountering these stories, and their fear is deeper and longer-lasting than that of a man; women are simply more engaged. Second, 'women may enjoy reading these books because they learn survival tips and strategies'. For example, true crime often dives into the motivation behind the actions of a murderer or a rapist (see pages 246–7) and can give women tools to identify the same in their everyday lives.

And in 2018, the Americans Kelli Boling and Kevin Hull penned a paper where they noticed that women were far more motivated by voyeurism than men. Women were reported as saying, 'Listening to true crime podcasts allows me to get a peek into a criminal mind,' and 'I enjoy listening to true crime podcasts because I like hearing about the secrets or misdeeds of someone's life.' Voyeurism is no small motivator. It's made *Big Brother* a hit, and we all like to people-watch now and then. But criminal voyeurism also includes a certain frisson. The empathy of *imagining* yourself inside the world of a true crime documentary is exciting.

Of course, no one person is the same, and there's no single reason anyone likes a true crime documentary. But millions of people do. In some ways, it mirrors our innate curiosity about the darker aspects of human nature. Just as we might slow down to look at a car accident, we're drawn to the details of a crime, compelled by a mix of empathy, fear and fascination.

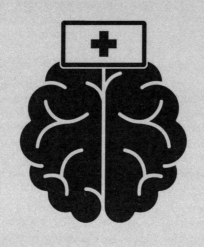

Health Psychology

*When you hear someone say, 'It's all in the mind,'
they're usually trying to trivialise an experience. You
can get over this pain; pain is only a construct of your
brain. As this book hopefully shows, everything is in the
mind. It's not just pain. When it comes to health, our
psychology is often just as important as our biology.*

*Health psychology is about our attitudes and
behaviours towards illness and health.*

Engel

The Whole Patient

Somewhere on your body, right now, there is an itch. Pause for a moment. Look away from this page. Focus on your body and find that itch. Scratch it if you want. Within seconds, there'll be another itch waiting for you. At every moment of the day, our bodies demand scratching. But we don't spend all our waking seconds clawing at ourselves like a dog in need of a cone. Our mind focuses on other things. Our body prioritises.

This one example highlights how complex it is to diagnose anything to do with the body.

In 1977, the American psychiatrist George Engel claimed there was 'a crisis in the biomedical paradigm'. Engel highlighted the fact that the biomedical model, which saw disease in terms of biological or neurological causes, left out a lot about a patient's life. When a GP meets a patient, they will often perform a biomedical test – they'll peer down your throat, look into your ears, monitor your blood pressure and so on. These tests will either point towards some diagnostics or lead to a referral for higher-order biomedical checks, like blood tests and MRI scans. For the majority of cases, this works perfectly well.

But here's a curious fact: between 20 and 30 per cent of all hospital outpatients have no discernible or obvious biomedical pathology. There is no immediate medical reason why a quarter of all patients are admitted to the hospital. Why, then, do some people think they are ill or claim 'symptoms' when there's no biological basis for that? Two examples:

A middle-aged woman appears at the hospital with heart palpitations, chest pain and dizziness. Tests come back with nothing. It turns out she's been working on three hours of sleep a night to meet a high-stress deadline at work.

A young man claims to have severe nausea and headaches. Scans reveal nothing medically wrong with him. It turns out the man is deeply traumatised by his childhood, and he experiences these symptoms when he has any kind of interaction with his family.

Engel's 'biopsychosocial' model is designed to explain examples like these. This model looks at biomedical causes *alongside* psychological and social factors. As part of this, Engel advocated for a more holistic approach to patient care, where doctors consider the patient's entire life situation. For example, a person suffering from heart disease might benefit from medical treatment (biological), stress management techniques (psychological) and community support or rehabilitation programmes (social).

The biopsychosocial model has hugely influenced medical education and practice, encouraging healthcare professionals to adopt a more patient-centred approach. During any 'first contact' medical interviews, a good doctor will often not only inquire about symptoms but also the patient's personal story, emotional wellbeing and social context, aiming for an effective healthcare experience.

(I hope this chapter has distracted you enough from those itches.)

Lazarus and Folkman
How to Deal with Stress

Stress is a normal and everyday part of our lives. If someone tells you they've never been stressed about anything, they're either lying or a Shaolin monk. An unavoidable part of life is that we will meet challenges and obstacles. We will have to get out of bed, put in a shift, and get a sweat on once in a while. To live is to struggle, at least sometimes.

But some people crumple under the tiniest hint of stress and others can load it on their broad shoulders and walk twenty miles. What makes stress bearable for some and crippling for others?

For an answer to this, we have Richard Lazarus and Susan Folkman's theory of stress and coping.

Lazarus and Folkman's approach begins by borrowing a little CBT and Stoic wisdom. They argue that no event in life is stressful *in itself*, but rather it *becomes* stressful when we appraise it that way. Stress is a feeling that emerges from the very particular relationship between the person and the environment. It's when someone decides that a certain life event goes beyond the resources they have to cope. A poor night's sleep is bad. But it's not stressful until it becomes something bigger. A week of bad nights, a year of insomnia, and sleeplessness become stressful. People say, 'I can't go on like this.'

Lazarus and Folkman called this the primary appraisal stage, where we reflect on a negative life experience and conclude it is either positive ('No pain, no gain'), irrelevant ('Ah, it's only one night's sleep) or stressful ('I can't do my job like this'). We then form a secondary appraisal stage where we gather our forces and make a battle plan. We ask, first, 'Can I cope with this?' then, 'If not, what do I need?' Not everyone is well suited to secondary appraisal, especially in the heat of the moment, and it might require help – professional or otherwise – to elicit the response.

Then we have the most important part: coping. All stress, no matter how bad, can be resolved with two kinds of coping mechanisms. The first, known as 'problem-focused' coping, is to find the source of the problem and remove it. If you're stressed about your finances, getting a better-paid job would fix the issue. Sometimes, though, the problem cannot be easily resolved, so we resort to 'emotion-focused' coping. This is where we accept that the issue won't go away and develop strategies to deal with it. We meditate, go to the gym or have a massive blow-out at the weekend.

Ironically, it's easy to get stressed about stress. And Lazarus and Folkman can help with that. Whenever you next go through a stressful period, their rationalisation can help put it in perspective and give you the tools to deal with it, as you've done so many times before.

Seligman

Okay is Not Okay

A lot of people have some kind of mental illness. According to some, that's a sign of our times. But it's likely because we're much better at identifying, recording and addressing mental illnesses than we used to be. You probably know someone with anxiety, OCD or depression. You might even suffer from them yourself. These days, those with mental health conditions go to a doctor, seek therapy or take medication.

Despite the huge increase in awareness and the raw numbers of those diagnosed, it's still true that the vast majority of people do *not* have a mental health condition. But that doesn't mean everyone's happy. There is a large, forgotten majority who lurk between 'I love life!' and the mentally ill. These are the people who are simply getting by. They're coping. They're middling along, doing all right, and feel just a bit 'meh' about life generally.

It was this fact and these people that Martin Seligman sought to address with his 'positive psychology'.

Seligman believed that psychology needed to expand its focus. Yes, pathology, victimology and mental illness are important, but so too is the study of positive human functioning. We should not only look to restore the damaged but also focus on the strengths and virtues that enable individuals and communities to flourish. After all, we're meant to thrive, not just survive. We should be proactive, not reactive.

Seligman introduced the 'PERMA' model, a five-step guide to increasing happiness and wellbeing. Try it yourself. Rank yourself 1–5 on the following:

- *Positive feelings*: How often do you feel happy, joyful and grateful? How often do you pause to recognise your feelings?

- *Engagement*: How often do you give your entire attention to a task or activity? Playing with your kids, riding a bike, watching nature and so on?

- *Relationships*: How many good friends or family members do you have that you speak to regularly? How many open, honest and profound conversations do you have a month?

- *Meaning*: What gets you out of bed in the morning? What excites you and motivates you to take action? If you died tomorrow, which project would you be sad to leave undone?

- *Achievement*: How often do you set goals and accomplish them? How often do you experience victory and achievement?

In many ways, we live in the post-Seligman age. Anyone who's been through a compulsory HR wellbeing meeting or sat through a headmaster's start of term talk (as either a parent or a teacher) will yawn at yet another mention of 'wellbeing'. But Seligman paved the way. He was the first to recognise that 'not bad' is not the same as happiness. Just because something's not broken doesn't mean it can't be fixed.

Selye
Learn When to Suffer

There is a burgeoning industry in misery-merchants, those self-help gurus or wellbeing books which tell us that 'suffering does you good'. They will often cite Friedrich Nietzsche or Viktor Frankl, or, if they're more theologically inclined, Irenaeus and the Buddha will get a look-in, too. The idea is that hard times are an essential part of life. Embrace suffering. Welcome misery. It's always darkest before dawn.

There is a lot of truth in this. But that word 'suffering' does a lot of heavy lifting. For most people in the developed world, 'suffering' means the occasional illness or broken bone. It's a relationship break-up, temporary unemployment or bereavement. This can certainly mature us in the long run. But there's another kind of category altogether: traumatic, devastating and debilitating suffering.

According to the Hungarian-Canadian endocrinologist Hans Selye, the first type of suffering is an example of 'eustress'. Eustress has positive outcomes that allow us to grow and deepen. But some suffering is 'distress' and this can damage us. It leaves us with deep-rooted trauma.

When you first encounter a stressful experience, it's unclear whether it's eustress or distress. A short, didactic encounter with misery is good. But if you are forced to endure hardship for too long, then things turn bad. In his research, Selye identified three distinct stages of response to stress: alarm, resistance and exhaustion.

The *alarm reaction* is the first response to a stressor, and it activates your body's sympathetic nervous system. Imagine a young mother called Ana who lives in a city in a volatile country. She's feeding her children dinner when she hears a gunshot outside. Her heart rate soars as adrenaline floods her system, preparing her for fight or flight. Her breathing becomes rapid and shallow, increasing the oxygen supply to her muscles.

If the stressor persists, the body enters the *resistance stage*, during which it adapts to the stressor through physiological changes. If the guns continue, Ana pushes down her immediate reaction and takes care of business. She gets her kids to the safest room possible, and she soothes them. She is not so full of adrenaline, but her heart is still racing, and she is still hyper-alert.

If the stress persists beyond the body's capacity to cope, it enters the *exhaustion stage*, leading to a depletion of resources, decreased stress tolerance and potential health problems. It's been three months now, and there are gunshots all the time. Ana has been on alert for nearly a month, and she's exhausted. She's grown used to it, but no one ever really gets used to living in a war zone.

Recognising the difference between eustress and distress is crucial to managing our wellbeing. Not all suffering is good. Sometimes pain is a learning experience and other times it destroys us. Sometimes it makes us; sometimes it breaks us.

Leventhal

Is It Bad, Doc?

Gregor is an oncology consultant. On any given day, he will have to deliver life-changing news to strangers. He will have to tell a mother that her daughter has leukaemia. A rich businessman that he has testicular cancer. An old lady that she has only a few months to live.

Over his twenty years in the job, Gregor has noticed that there are different types of patients. When people listen to Gregor give an earth-shattering diagnosis, they behave differently. Patient A knows about cancer, knows their human biology, and asks certain intellectually challenging questions. Patient B had a brother survive cancer, so he asks questions about treatment plans and length. Patient C has no idea what cancer really is and no idea about the statistics. They don't even know if or how much they should be worried.

Gregor is observing what the American psychologist Howard Leventhal has theorised over his years of studying patients at the point of diagnosis. It's because of Leventhal that doctors often talk to you the way they do.

At the heart of Leventhal's study of 'illness perception' is the idea that illness is not merely a biological phenomenon but a psychological experience. This experience is filtered through a variety of personal beliefs about the nature of the illness, its causes, its duration and its potential impact on one's life. These beliefs, in turn, influence the strategies individuals employ to cope with their condition, whether through rigorous adherence to treatment and engagement in health-promoting behaviours, or through denial and avoidance.

Leventhal's 'self-regulation model' of illness perception identifies five key dimensions shaping how we each respond to an illness: identity (the label and symptoms of the illness); cause (personal beliefs about what led to the illness); timeline (how long the individual believes the illness will last); consequences (expected effects of the illness on one's life); and controllability (the extent to which the individual believes the illness can be managed or cured).

So, let's suppose a smoker has been diagnosed with lung cancer. They can identify the disease and know its cause – they've seen it on the cigarette packets. But this patient has no idea how long the cancer will last or how lethal it might be. Any doctor diagnosing this patient needs to establish the patient's level of knowledge across all five areas.

Leventhal's research has not only found its way into the consultant's room. It applies to public health as well. Much of the work around vaccine uptake, for instance, is about developing education around these five categories. Conversely, stigma about or fear of a disease (which often exacerbates it, not least for those avoiding getting checked out) relies on ignorance and hearsay.

It's not reaching too far to say that Leventhal's work has transformed an area of life we will all, one day, experience. It will change how we face our own mortality.

Kabat-Zinn

Chewing a Raisin

You've been invited to dinner at a friend's house, where they've prepared a lovely lamb tagine. You all sit down at your places, ladle out your portions and tuck in. Halfway through dinner, you suddenly notice something odd has happened to the person sitting across from you: she has completely stopped talking and is staring at you with the dead eyes of a Halloween mannequin.

'Are you all right?' you ask, a touch nervously. She jumps, as if you've broken her reverie.

'Oh, sorry,' she says. 'I'm trying mindful eating. I'm focusing on every bite.'

I will bet my mala beads that you've heard of mindfulness. It's our modern-day mental health fad – and it's a fad that works. Of course, mindfulness has been around for millennia. It's found in the Indian Vedas, Greek philosophy and indigenous worship all around the world. The first prehistoric human who said, 'Gah! I'm angry; I'm going out for a walk,' was getting into mindfulness. But it's only fairly recently that the secular and psychological communities have put mindfulness on all of our lips.

In the late 1970s, Jon Kabat-Zinn founded the Mindfulness-Based Stress Reduction (MBSR) programme, which combines mindfulness meditation and yoga to help individuals cope with stress, pain and illness. It asks participants to experience moment-to-moment awareness and non-judgemental acceptance of their experiences. MBSR and mindfulness more broadly offer two beneficial outcomes: the first is that we enjoy the moment more and can relax into the stillness of the present. Second, though, is a wisdom that we've already come across (see pages 16–19): if you take stock of your own feelings you can take control of them.

There is a famous MBSR exercise involving a raisin. First, you hold the raisin in your hand. Explore it with your eyes, nose and fingers. Encounter the raisin with each of your senses. After a while, pop the raisin in your mouth. Do not bite. Notice how your mouth changes shape and how you salivate (page 156). Appreciate the automatic actions your body runs through. Finally, you can chew. Do so slowly and thoughtfully. Which teeth do you use? What tastes are there? How does your tongue move the raisin? Finally, acknowledge the urge to swallow. Why then? What does an urge feel like? Then, swallow. Imagine the hidden, bilious onward journey of your friend, the desiccated grape.

Of course, no one with a life can carry on like this all the time, but the point of mindfulness and MBSR is to appreciate that all things in life can be broken down and enjoyed this way. Sometimes, this is enough to slow down a frenetic, anxious mind. Sometimes, it might be a way to turn boredom into calm. The great thing about MBSR is that you can take it with you wherever you are – a portable, effective trick.

Taylor

New Mums and Pre-season Fitness

You've probably heard of the 'fight or flight' response (some add 'freeze' as a third option). Common wisdom states that when most animals are faced with a threat, they will either lash out with tooth and claw (fight) or hotfoot it to safety (flight). For a lot of people, especially in acute, sudden moments of perceived danger (like seeing a huge spider in the shower next to you), this holds true. But it also misses out on another aspect of human nature: our ability to huddle together. When things get hard – the relentless hard of grief, loneliness or sustained stress – people might withdraw. They isolate themselves, and in the cold corridors of isolation, depression often lurks. Some people, though, will reach out. They'll form strong and lasting bonds with others, often from quite surprising walks of life.

This is known as Shelley Taylor's 'tend and befriend' theory.

Oddly, Taylor's idea contradicts another idea in this book (see Sherif, pages 126–7). It's sometimes supposed that when times are hard and resources are scarce, people turn on one another. Compassion is a luxury of prosperity, and humans are kind only so long as they're happy. But Taylor's research shows that when life goes through a rough patch, many people will first 'tend' to the most vulnerable (often the young) and 'befriend' others in similar situations. New parents, for example, will bond over the care of their children and are often surprised by the depth of connection with other parents they meet. The reason groups like the NCT and antenatal classes are so popular reflects Taylor's observation: new parents need to stick together because it gets pretty rough in the sleep-deprived, vomit-smelling, screaming nightmare of the soft-play years.

Of course, it's not just new parents. Pre-season fitness sessions for a sports club are not only good for your aerobic fitness, they're also good for team spirit. A team in the office, working to a deadline on a big project, comes together and probably celebrates a bit too hard in the pub at the end. A community is often brought together by tragedy. A nation is brought together by war.

Taylor's original research suggested that 'tend and befriend' is more common with women, which is partially a socialised behaviour and also has to do with female-specific reproductive hormones. But in 2019, Kenneth N. Levy et al. showed that it might be more to do with 'attachment styles' (see pages 34–5) than gender differences. Either way, Taylor's theory is another reminder – a reminder that pops up again and again in this book – that we need one another. Problems are multiplied alone, and some things in life are so relentless and overwhelming that they will drown you if you don't have others to pull you up.

Pender

Why You're Not Healthy

What we consider 'normal' is almost entirely defined by the people around us. If all of your family is loud and chatty, it might seem abnormal to eat in silence. If your friends all swear like sailors, it will feel weird to talk to someone who's precious about it. Nowhere is this normalisation more prevalent than in our attitudes towards health. Consider these questions:

What does a normal body size look like to you?

What's a normal and acceptable amount to drink every week?

How many people do you know who smoke or vape?

The answers to those questions will likely determine your own attitude towards obesity, alcohol and smoking. People who are only slightly overweight won't see themselves as overweight if surrounded by the clinically obese.

This fact is one of the key elements of Nola Pender's popular and often-used Health Promotion Model (HPM).

Pender's handbook for inducing healthy lifestyle habits hinges on the single assumption that most people want to improve themselves and their environment. We all want to be better and healthier. The problem, though, is that there are obstacles in the way that prevent this. The logic, then, is that if we remove these obstacles people's natural tendency to want to be well will kick in. Pender identified three barriers in the way.

1. *Individual characteristics and experiences*: These are the values and beliefs you have already, based upon prior experience; for example, if you've never eaten a tasty salad, then that will inform your eating habits. But it's also your inherited characteristics, like an addictive personality, and your acquired ones, like being surrounded with friends who all smoke.

2. *Behavioural-specific cognitions*: These are the mental and emotional barriers that influence behaviour. For example, we might be scared of going to the gym or feel that preparing fresh meals is too expensive and time-consuming. It's also about self-efficacy, where people feel defeatist or weak-willed. 'It's too late for me, anyway.'

3. *Behavioural outcomes*: If Pender is right that we all *want* to be healthy, we also have to know what it is that makes us healthy. We have to set accurate and true outcomes. If someone thinks a ten-minute walk counteracts a full English, they're misinformed.

The HPM needs no defining when you work in public health or nursing communities. It's been widely adopted for medical research, education and practice and has been proven to be effective in changing unhealthy behaviours and promoting health. So, if you're feeling a bit flabby or want to quit a bad habit (see pages 218–19), then work your way down Pender's list of obstacles and resolve them. Your body wants to be healthy, so let it.

Everyday Psychology
The Effects of a Pandemic

Before 2020, the last major pandemic in the UK was the Spanish flu 100 years ago. Which means that there are only a handful of people alive today old enough to remember what that was like. Then, the world got COVID-19, the pandemic of the century, with a 3 per cent fatality rate in the general population and three times higher for the vulnerable and elderly. Countries all over the world went into lockdown. The first duty of a government is to protect its citizens, so they introduced measures to save as many as possible. At first, lockdown was a novelty. A week without leaving your house might be boring if you're alone, relaxing if you're a couple and hair-tearingly stressful if you're a parent. But it was bearable. Then days turned to weeks, weeks turned to months, and Christmas in a bubble wasn't all that festive.

Now, with the dust just starting to settle on our COVID-19 testing packs, psychologists are examining what a pandemic does to our minds.

At the end of 2020, an international team of psychologists, biologists and sociologists produced a systemic review of how much damage lockdown did to our mental health. Unsurprisingly, people were vastly more anxious, depressed and lonely than they were pre-pandemic. These are some of the paper's findings.

First, there was the impact the news had. News always leans towards the miserable, scary and salacious ('Everything is okay!' won't sell a newspaper), but COVID-19 was another thing altogether. Every day, media outlets were pushing fear. This isn't to say it was needlessly exaggerated – the dangers of COVID-19 were very real – but seeing a daily death toll understandably makes people anxious.

Second, there was the uncertainty. Humans tend to enjoy novel experiences – for a while. Not only did people not know when the lockdown would end but they didn't know if they'd still have a job or if their loved ones would survive. Some people wondered if *they* would survive. If you live with uncertainty for long enough, it wears you down.

Third, there was the loneliness. One 2020 study by Groarke et al. said that nearly a third of people in the UK felt desperately alone during the lockdown. The most at-risk were the young, recently separated or divorced, depressed, highly emotional and insomniac (see page 274). The anxiety and stress of lockdown were bad for everyone, but they were amplified for the lonely. And behind their locked doors, the lonely and scared became depressed.

We still do not know the long-term psychological implications of the pandemic, but early evidence suggests that they will be legion. The choice to enforce a lockdown was based on a cost-benefit analysis for the general population. With the costs still piling up with every new study, it's an open question how governments will respond to the next pandemic.

Walker

An Hour Before Midnight is Worth Two After

If you've ever been seriously sleep-deprived, you will already know how strange the world can seem. If you've come off an overnight flight with twenty minutes of neck-cramping sleep, you'll be familiar with the ethereal disconnect of the arrivals lounge. If you've got a young baby and haven't slept well for three months, you'll know how easy it is to stare, unblinkingly, at a blank wall. Serious sleep deprivation changes how your mind works.

It's a curious and humbling fact that almost all of our cognitive faculties depend on getting at least a few hours of sleep every night. Without it, we find it hard to think straight. We forget things quicker. We are less empathetic, grumpier and far, far less patient with fools. The fact that sleep is important is obvious to anyone who's gone without it, but recently, in his book *Why We Sleep*, the British psychologist Matthew Walker talked us through just *how* important it is.

Although Walker writes about how sleep affects our attention, emotional states and overall health, he focuses most on how sleep affects our memory. Sleep is important in all three areas of learning: acquisition, storage and recall.

As we go about our daily lives, our brains are constantly jotting things down. A brain encodes all its new information by conceptualising it, then putting it aside for later. When we sleep, our brain assimilates our experiences. It gets the canvas ready for the paint of the day. Without sleep, though, the canvas is a tiny, dirty sackcloth that can barely take in anything.

When we sleep, the mind goes to town on the day's events. As we dream of silly nonsense, our hippocampus is filing our experiences into 'useless', 'useful' and 'too early to tell'. It lays down the good stuff into short-term memories and flushes out the inessential to make room for tomorrow. Walker's studies show that if people stay awake for more than sixteen hours then the hippocampus doesn't have enough time to get its job done. Your memories will leak away in an insomniac slush.

Finally, during sleep, the brain will move short-term memories into the brain's cortex, where they will take residence in our long-term memory. It's because of sleep that you can remember your first boyfriend, the first time you drank alcohol, and the panting face of your childhood dog. It's depressing to wonder how many memories are lost to you because you didn't sleep well. It also explains why a big night out is often hazy; drunken sleep is poor sleep, and the hippocampus doesn't stand a chance.

Sleep is the most abused and underappreciated of all essential bodily needs. We've all pulled an all-nighter in our time, or stayed up too late doing nothing good. Walker's book teaches us that we need to prioritise sleep for our health, just as we do with exercising and eating well.

Experimental Psychology

Everyone does psychology with a small p. It's the basis of empathy, communication and theory of mind (knowing what people are thinking). When someone says, 'Do you think he likes me?' or 'Why the hell did Mum say that?', they're doing psychology. But psychology as a discipline will often need more (although many in this book are guilty of not doing that much more). Psychology needs funding, experimentation, data and replicability. All of which are often hard to find and hard to do.

Experimental psychology is about doing psychology as a study.

Watson

How to Take Psychology Seriously

I mean, this book has been nice and everything, and I'm sure people are having a great time studying it at universities around the world, but psychology is all a load of waffle, isn't it? The neuroscience stuff isn't that bad, but that's basically biology or medicine. The rest is just a load of people making up random theories. Whenever they actually do decide to empirically test their theories, they're either impossible to replicate (see page 133) or inconclusive. Psychoanalysis is no different from religion, social psychology is boringly obvious, and forensic psychology has more critics than theorists. But the biggest problem of all is that psychology deals with subjective human thoughts in private minds. Introspection (pages 16–17), mindfulness (page 267) and emotional conceptualisation (pages 110–111) are all very well, but they're based on self-reporting, untestable anecdotes. Good for a theory, but bad science.

This is the basic starting point of John B. Watson's behaviourism.

For Watson, psychology can only be concerned with recordable, observable human behaviours. Any 'science' that depends on internal phenomena will always deteriorate into quackery or, worse, philosophy. So, if psychologists can only concern themselves with measurable actions, what do they focus on? Environmental factors. For Watson, the single most important factor – if not the *only* factor – determining personality, cognition, emotion or learning is our environment. We are the product of the world pressing down on us.

This is why Watson, and behaviourism more broadly, took such a keen interest in conditioning. Like Ivan Pavlov (pages 174–5) and B. F. Skinner (pages 24–5), Watson believed that learning is a process of conditioning. All of our behaviours are the result of associations between stimuli and responses, which are reinforced or punished depending on their consequences. A human mind is a mixture of mirror and sponge. We reflect back what we're told and we take in what we see.

There is a notorious Jesuit expression that goes: 'Give me a child until he is seven and I will give you the man.' Watson would likely have nodded his head approvingly. But there is a darker side to behaviourism. In Anthony Burgess's book *A Clockwork Orange*, the sociopathic criminal Alex is conditioned to feel physically sick at the thought of violence. In *The Giver* by Lois Lowry, people are conditioned to experience only anodyne feelings known as 'Sameness'. In George Orwell's *1984*, 2 + 2 = 5.

But dystopian brainwashing is not only what conditioning is about. Every human, everywhere, has been conditioned by their upbringing. A philanthropist is 'made' as much as a criminal. A conservative and a liberal, Christian and Muslim, vegetarian and carnivore, racist and egalitarian are all, equally, the product of their environments. Behaviourism recognises that the only reason you're reading this page is because of the maze that led you here.

Rosenthal

Finding What You're Looking for

In 2017, the American psychologist Jean Twenge wrote an article for *The Atlantic* called 'Have Smartphones Destroyed a Generation?' And it went stratospherically viral. Everyone and their dog retweeted it, and schools up and down the country scrambled to add 'screentime' to their PSHE lessons. Twenge's arguments fell on receptive ears. People were ready to believe that screens caused depression, anxiety and the end of civilisation.

The problem, though, is that Twenge's research is hugely controversial. It's almost certainly misleading. The data Twenge calls upon is vast – hundreds of thousands of participants rating and ranking things across hundreds of aspects of life. And, yes, in that data, it shows a very small correlation between screen use and depression. So is Twenge right? Well, yes, but she also left out some other important correlations. People who ate more potatoes showed just as large an increase in depression risk. Those who wear glasses are far, far more likely to be depressed than both the smartphone and potato statistics show.

The problem was that Twenge was looking for a certain effect. She came with a hypothesis in mind. She's possibly guilty of the 'experimenter effect'.

In the 1960s, the German-born American psychologist Robert Rosenthal gave two groups of scientists the same rats and the same mazes. He told one group the rats were bred for maze competence, and the other group were told the rats were bred for maze stupidity. What Rosenthal noted was that each group found and noted far more data that confirmed their pre-existing hypotheses. The rats were the same.

Rosenthal's study has been replicated again and again, and it's intuitively obvious. It's essentially confirmation biases of the Pygmalion effect (see pages 184–5) in a lab coat. People will see what they want to see. This has led the scientific community to employ 'double-blind' experiments where possible. This is where both the participants and researchers don't know who is given a treatment or intervention, so they will, as accurately as possible, monitor objective behaviours. In a world of computer learning and imminent AI integration, it's even possible to remove human bias altogether.

Of course, not all experiments allow for double-blind conditions. It's hard for a surgeon and their patient to be ignorant of the scalpel cutting their thigh, for example. But Rosenthal is part of a group of meta-scientists who have cleaned up the scientific method more broadly. His research acts as a kind of checking mechanism to prevent psychology from giving way to confirmation bias.

Everyday Psychology
Good for the Soul, Good for Your Heart

There are few things as good for the soul as a long, breathless, unstoppable laugh. Laughter is good for your heart, good for your mental health and can serve as a pain reliever. Many species demonstrate laughter-like behaviour – chimpanzees, gorillas, bonobos, orangutans, rats, mice and dogs all have been recorded laughing. If you have three hours to kill, YouTube is packed with laughing animals.

And yet, for all that, we have no idea why we laugh. We do not know the evolutionary purpose of laughter, we don't know the social function of laughter, and we don't even know what biological functions induce laughter. But we have lots of theories. Here are some of the best.

The relief theory was a favourite of Sigmund Freud (see pages 14–15). Freud believed that a good joke will build up a kind of 'psychic energy', which is then dissipated, or relieved, by the joke's climax. Psychic energy sounds like a Dungeons and Dragons spell, but here it means only the pent-up emotion of expectation and suspense that a good joke leads you to. 'Why did the chicken cross the road?' sets you up to worry about the chicken, to mentally picture speeding cars, and to live with the tension of an unanswered question. As the comedian says, 'To get to the other side,' the relief funnels out as side-splitting laughter.

Given that Thomas Hobbes wrote a lot about fear, paranoia and domination (see page 27), it's unsurprising that he believed that all humour was a kind of power play. The superiority theory of humour states that we find something funny because we get to assert our will over it. We get to mock or ridicule something. We point and laugh at the butt of a joke, and laughter feels good because it means safety and power.

Finally, incongruity theory suggests that the essence of humour is resolving conflict or something that deviates from what is expected. 'Why did the invisible man turn down a job offer?' leads you to think it'll be about money, health or working conditions. When the punchline comes: 'Because he couldn't see himself doing it,' the joke makes an abrupt, incongruent turn. Chortles and back slaps all around.

And yet it doesn't take a stand-up comedian to realise that all three theories have as many exceptions as examples. Humour is a near universal aspect of the human condition, but *what* we find humorous will change from person to person, culture to culture, and era to era. The one thing we *do* know, though, is that laughter is good for you. It releases happy endorphins into the bloodstream, lowers stress hormones, decreases pain, relaxes muscles, prevents heart disease and boosts immunity. Don't just get a medical check-up; go to a comedy club.

Wundt
The Fluff of a Dog's Tail

The job of a good critic is to break down a piece of art into its component parts. They will take a movie, for example, and throw it on the dissector's table. They'll rip out the cinematography and carve out the musical score. They'll anatomise the cast and amputate the director's intentions. They'll hold up each piece to their honed, critical eye and tell you what's good and bad about it. Then they'll tell you how all the pieces hold together.

A car is the sum of its mechanics. A song is a collection of notes and lyrics. A football team has eleven players. Almost anything can be broken down into parts. According to Wilhelm Wundt, the mind is no different.

Wundt founded the first 'psychology laboratory' in Leipzig, Germany, in 1879, almost a decade before Freud (pages 14–15) wrote his most famous works. Which means that Wundt has a good case for not only being the father of experimental psychology (as he's often labelled), but the father of psychology as a whole. Sadly, like a lot of nineteenth-century science, Wundt's approach hasn't quite survived the test of time. Wundt was a structuralist, and he aimed to identify the basic building blocks of consciousness through introspection and reflection. His days were spent encouraging various trained observers to report their conscious experiences in response to stimuli.

'Hello, my friend,' Wundt might say. 'Here is a picture of a fluffy dog. Look at it. Enjoy it. So fluffy. So lovely. *Now tell me what's going on in your head right now.*'

There is a perception of a dog – the individual component sensations, like the fluff, big ears and tail – but also the gestalt of the entire dogginess (see pages 98–9). The dog holds our attention, and it creates a mental image. This evokes an emotional response based on the current environment and the unfamiliar, unmapped darkness of our upbringing. We form associations with the dog – hair-covered sofas, barking, dog poo and so on. Then we place the dog into wider categories, like 'animal' or 'pet' or 'friendly'.

All of that for a picture of a dog. Wundt tried to apply this kind of analysis to every single element of our mind. He focused mostly on sensations and perceptions and how they combine to form complex experiences, but also on how they affect all our other mental processes.

Structuralism eventually fell out of favour, mostly because people realised that the brain is such a hugely complex beast that it can't be simplified in the way Wundt wanted. Well, not without almost always misrepresenting or reducing the structure you're trying to understand. For all that, Wundt's contribution is huge, and he takes his rightful place in this book as the forgotten father of a discipline that was just finding its feet.

James
The Job of a Brain

When you spend a lot of time reading psychology books and talking about the brain, you'll notice a line pop up so often that you don't even think to challenge it: 'The brain is brilliant.' There's this narrative that the brain is the most incredible thing in the universe, rivalling the fundamental forces of physics. But let's get some perspective. Because behind all the billions of synapses and electrical-hormonal lobes is the simple fact that the brain is a tool. It's designed to help humans survive, have sex and pass on our genes. It's a weapon in the evolutionary toolbox – a weapon that has got us pretty far, to be fair.

This 'functionalist' view of the brain goes back to the nineteenth-century American thinker William James.

Cards on the table: James is one of my top three writers of all time, in terms of both style and content. He walks the frontier lands of psychology and philosophy, carrying an almanac of trivia and classical references, all of which he punctuates with winks and humour. So, when I say, 'William James is the father of modern psychology,' you should take it as my opinion and not a universally accepted fact. But he is certainly one of the first to make a proper and reputable science of psychology; in fact, he even took on Sigmund Freud for his decidedly unscientific views.

Over the course of his many lectures and books, James argues for a functionalist view of the mind, where mental processes are understood based on their role in adapting to the environment. The unity of consciousness, our cognitive processes and all our behaviours are geared towards helping us navigate our surroundings. It's in functionalism that we see the genesis of behavioural psychology, where sexual attraction, aggression, nesting and so on are all explained by their evolutionary function. For instance, we tend to find people attractive if they look healthy and have childbearing potential.

One of the most important elements of the brain's functionalism is its plasticity. Many later psychologists expanded on and proved the idea, but James was the first to suggest that the brain adapts to the environment you provide it – for example, if you spend years in Iceland (see pages 186–7), you'll find you learn to speak Icelandic and can differentiate types of geysers.

As with any tool, the brain is as good as the task you give it. And if you test, push and challenge the brain, it will rise to meet the task. So, yes, the brain is brilliant, but that's not only because of its raw power but also because of its adaptability. That allows us to deal with almost anything.

Everyday Psychology
The Olympic Model for Success

There are few things more trite, not to mention patently untrue, than the exhortations 'it's all mind over matter' or 'you can do anything you put your mind to'. Well, no, some people can't do certain things. However much I run the odd lap around the park, I'm never going to win the New York marathon by gumption alone. Simply wanting something does not make it so.

A study involving Swiss cyclists showed that biology (for example, a person's VO_2 max) accounted for roughly 75 per cent of an athlete's performance. Which means only 25 per cent is down to mindset and willpower. Swimmers need long arms, weightlifters need to be mesomorphs and jockeys need to be tiny. Bodies do matter when it comes to elite sports.

Forgive me if you're reading this in the Olympic village, but for the rest of us wheezing, wobbly amateurs, psychology is *much* more important. In 2018, the Canadian sports psychologist Natalie Durand-Bush looked at all the existing studies and data and developed a 'Gold-Silver-Bronze' model for a successful mindset.

The Gold mental traits are motivation, confidence and resilience. You have to desperately want to get better, win a race or secure your personal best. If you're only doing something because of external pressure, your motivation will falter. Confidence is saying, 'I can lift this weight', or 'I can swim a mile'. It's the self-assured self-belief that doesn't register defeat. Related to confidence is resilience. When you do suffer defeat or a setback, you get back up again. If Louise in the Bristol office beats you in the triathlon, you embark on a *Rocky*-montage training year to make sure it doesn't happen again.

The Silver characteristics are all about emotional regulation. You need to have the self-awareness to appreciate when you train best, what went wrong and how to improve. But also, you need to be aware of your emotions. Are you burned out? Do you have a coping mechanism? How many times have you checked Louise's training times this week?

Finally, the Bronze is about the external environment that helps you achieve success. It might be getting a good coach who knows when to shout at you and when to give you a supportive pat. It might be learning to work as a team and joining a club – bending your own ambitions to the collective's.

Durand-Bush's Gold-Silver-Bronze model is about sports, but it doesn't take much squinting to see how it can apply to other aspects of life. A good doctor needs to be motivated and resilient; a good dad needs to have adequate coping mechanisms; and a good employee knows when to work alone and when to collaborate. As in sport, so in life.

Ebbinghaus
Learning Curves

When I was eighteen years old, I decided to learn the books of the Bible by rote. I admit, it's a niche and peculiar thing to do, but we all have our idiosyncrasies. I spent days repeating the list until eventually I could recite all sixty-six books, ready to impress my very unimpressed friends. If you asked me to list them today, I could probably name a few, and they'd probably be in the wrong order.

Over the years, my memory faded. I was, inexplicably, never asked to recite the books of the Bible enough. I didn't consolidate and reinforce my rote learning, and so my mostly useless trivia faded away. Of course, it's not just peculiar niches that fade. If you think back to your school days, how much do you remember now? Find a past paper online and see how many maths GCSE questions you can get right.

The fact is, if you don't pay attention to your memories, they'll leave you. Use them or lose them. And this is exactly what the German psychologist Hermann Ebbinghaus wanted to learn more about.

In the happy Wild West of nineteenth-century science, before control groups, randomised trials and double-blind procedures (see page 281), there was

Ebbinghaus, doing experiments on himself in his front room. Ebbinghaus created a list of roughly 2,000 'nonsense syllables', consisting of memorable sounds with no associations. So, he wouldn't have allowed HUT or FED if he were English but POB or ZON would be fine. Then, to the beat of a metronome, he would recite the syllables over and over again. He would learn them by rote.

From all this, Ebbinghaus gave us two very important ideas: the forgetting curve and the learning curve. The forgetting curve is the theory that memory loss is sharpest in the first twenty minutes after learning something, and then it roughly halves in the first hour. After a day or so, it plateaus somewhat but can bump about depending on lifestyle factors like stress or sleep. So, if you learned twenty nonsense syllables, you'd remember roughly ten in an hour and three or so in a week.

The learning curve is perhaps more useful. It tells us that learning is likewise exponential to forgetting. The sharpest learning happens during the first try or exposure, but we retain less and less after each time. Ebbinghaus theorised that the most effective way to retain a memory is by using the 'spacing effect'. So, rather than cramming information in a short burst, you need to revise and return to a memory over a series of days and weeks. Buck the curve by constantly propping it up along the way.

Which means, there's only one thing for it: I'm going to have to recite the books of the Bible to my family. (Divorce papers incoming.)

Tolman

It's All Going in Somewhere

The concept of 'sleep learning' has been with us for a long time. The idea is that while you snore away, dreaming of sweet nothings, your brain is idle and bored. You're wasting precious hours of the day, and your brain is craving stimulation and learning. So, as you sleep, put on an audiobook, and learn something! Listen to three hours of Victor Hugo in the original French or a 'how to quit smoking' guide. Sadly, sleep learning has had its day. Not only is it entirely ineffective but it turns out our brains are surprisingly busy as we sleep (see pages 274–5).

But the *theory* behind sleep learning is sound. That idea that some ideas are 'going in somewhere' and they might just come out again, one day. This is Edward Tolman's 'latent learning'.

According to traditional behaviourist models of learning based on Ivan Pavlov's (see pages 174–5) and B. F. Skinner's (see pages 24–5) ideas of classical conditioning, we are most likely to remember things when there is some kind of reinforcement mechanism. It might be an exam to study for or a pub quiz to win, but most people learn best when there's something to work towards.

But Tolman's work on rats revealed a chink in the behaviourist armour. Tolman put a group of rats into a maze and gave them no reinforcement whatsoever. They were free to get lost and meander as they pleased. After several days, Tolman then gave the rats rewards (reinforcement) if they completed the maze. What he found was that, almost overnight, the rats that had seemingly been wandering aimlessly worked out the maze. They were far quicker at doing so than rats who joined only at the reinforcement stage.

All this means that the no-reinforcement rats had built a mental map of the maze without any incentive whatsoever. They'd learned *without* reinforcement – something behaviourists didn't think possible. Somewhere in their ratty unconscious, Tolman's subjects had formed a 'cognitive map' of the maze, which came in very handy when they *did* get rewards. Tolman called this 'latent learning'.

While the idea of latent learning and cognitive maps has evolved considerably since Tolman's original 1930 study, the general concept has not changed much. Everything you learn or see is stored somewhere. Most of it gets swept away in the daily RAM-wipe of the mind, but the rest lingers around. And when Wilder Penfield (see pages 170–171) redrew the map of the brain, it became established wisdom that it really does all go in somewhere. We know more than we think.

Schachter and Singer
What Makes a Feeling a Feeling?

Let's play a game of 'What am I?' Here goes:

I make the amygdala activate the hypothalamus, initiating the hypothalamic-pituitary-adrenal axis response. This leads to the release of corticotropin-releasing hormone from the hypothalamus, which in turn stimulates the pituitary gland to secrete adrenocorticotropic hormone. ACTH prompts the adrenal glands to release cortisol. Concurrently, I activate the sympathetic nervous system, resulting in the release of epinephrine and norepinephrine.

Did you get it? Well, that's fear.

... But that isn't fear, is it? That's a list of hormones and neurochemicals. It's a biological, physicalist explanation of a feeling that we all have daily. When I experience 'fear', I know it's fear. I recognise it as fear. I say, 'Ah, yes, I'm terrified of this huge spider. I should probably run away.'

This is why Stanley Schachter and Jerome E. Singer's 'two-factor theory of emotion' is so important. Schachter and Singer argued that for an emotion to be called an emotion it needs two things. First, it needs the physiological arousal. It needs the adrenaline, cortisol and so on. Second, though, it requires a 'cognitive label'. It needs me to recognise what's happening in my body as a certain emotion. I need to label cortisol as stress or fear.

Schachter and Singer proved this with their 'epinephrine study' (in fact, it's so famous in psychological circles it's often called the Schachter and Singer Experiment and everyone is assumed to understand). In this 1962 study, participants were injected with either epinephrine, a hormone known to induce physiological arousal, or a placebo. The participants were then placed alongside an actor who feigned either happiness or anger at something. Without being told what they had been injected with, the participants overwhelmingly labelled their *own* emotion in line with the actor's. They knew they were having some feeling, but they called it anger or happiness depending on their environmental cues.

Not only have follow-up studies confirmed Schachter and Singer's original 1960s experiment but it's anecdotally corroborated all the time. If you feel jittery and have a racing heart, you might think you're nervous about a Zoom meeting later. In fact, you had too much coffee. If you're sweating and your palms are clammy before a big presentation, you might think it's anxiety. But maybe the room is just unusually warm from a broken radiator.

Philosophers and psychologists both love to riff on idea that it's good to 'know thyself' and be aware of your own inner life. What Schachter and Singer proved, though, is the 'self' that you know, and the inner life you see, depend partially on your environment and socialisation. You need to be *taught* to feel an emotion.

Everyday Psychology
Beware Pseudo-psychology

Psychology is a broad discipline. It ranges from CAT-scanning, diagram-loving neuroscientists all the way to Austrian neurologists, who had a few ideas. But it always tries to at least hover near the best available evidence. Psychoanalysis might not be as scientifically rigorous as a chemistry laboratory, but it does, in the main, bow to data and experiment. Sadly, the same cannot be said for a lot of popular psychology. Many newspapers and media outlets are guilty of leading with headlines that might be good for a click but almost always stray beyond the actual evidence.

A great example of this, and a cautionary tale for any would-be psychologist, is the field of 'colour psychology'.

There have been a lot of experiments over the years about why we like certain colours and what that can tell us about our personalities. Here's what we *do* know. First, some colours can nudge your behaviour (see page 297). For instance, people tend to donate more to logos or webpages coloured blue compared with red. Second, some colours can affect your mood to a degree. In 2015, a team from Melbourne found that 'students who glanced at a greener vista demonstrated superior concentration … compared to those who viewed a concrete roof'. Third, companies know that we associate colours with things. Red is good for 'call to action' buttons because it catches the eye. Pink is used for women's products.

But that's all we know. Even those three observations are based on limited studies with unrepeatable results and enough confounding factors to make even the computer game debate look clear-cut (see pages 240–1). There are so many unknown variables. 'Red makes people angry' might be true, or is there a third factor underpinning both? Does 'green' relax you, or is it that natural things like trees and meadows are green and also relaxing?

Most importantly, how we associate colours differs from culture to culture (see pages 210–11). In the West, red might signify danger, love or Christmas; in Southeast Asia, red is used in celebrations for its association with luck. In India, orange is sacred; in Egypt, it's the colour of grief. For me, blue might evoke the ocean, but for a Catholic in Mexico, it might mean the Virgin Mary. Even *within* a culture, colour association changes. For instance, in the USA before the 1940s, it was pink that was thought to be a boys' colour, and blue was for girls.

The main problem, as with a lot of pseudo-scientific pop psychology, is that it's fun to say, 'I like red, so I'm a passionate man,' or, 'I paint my study orange to focus better,' but any reputable psychologist needs to toe the data line. The far more boring, but accurate, fact is that human psychology and personality are so incredibly complex that there aren't many generic conclusions we can draw.

Acknowledgements

In order for me to write *Mini Psychology*, I had to hide myself away in the tiny room at the back of the house, which we call the study. I had to put my life on pause. I had to drop everything. But, of course, life doesn't pause, and other people pick up what you've dropped. An army marches on its stomach; battles and books are won by logistics.

First, my wife, Tanya. She is the lattice which holds up our entire family. She is always there to hear me ramble and rant. She knows when to support me and when to tell me I'm being silly. I believe most people need both from time to time. She is the beautiful paradox that keeps me grounded and lets me fly.

Second, Mum and Dad. They are the reason for this book existing. They gave me both curiosity and the materials to sate it. Dad taught me to look out at the world, and my mum taught me to look inward. I love them.

Third, Nanny and Paps — Roman and Ann — for helping not only by looking after my two boys but by turning them into the perfect little humans they are. They have always been there and will always be there. Their kindness shines, and our house is brighter.

Fourth, my brother. I genuinely think no relationship is as deeply etched as that of a sibling. They are the ones who have seen you grow, cry and laugh. They understand those private jokes and obscure references that no one else does or could. I've always hero-worshipped my brother. He is a hero.

Finally, Lindsay, my editor, who had to put up with yet another round of bad jokes, bad grammar and first-draft illustrations that look like turds.

Then there is the entire cast of loved ones who will, undoubtedly, resent not getting their own paragraph. There's Ellen — the kind of gentle, genuine human it's impossible to dislike. James, Hagir, and Jonny — the family to which I cling. Stephen — technically my boss, lovingly my mate. Charlie — my agent and spirit guide in the publishing world.

Last, there's Ellie, Wally, Lisa, Claire H, Rosa, Traff, Abi, Emma, Joe, Matt, Emma, Claire O, Henry, Hannah and Tom. All of whom have been there to pick me up and put me back. All of which feature as examples in this book, often pseudonymously. I hope they spend at least some time agonising over where.

Index

Index

Index